S0-BJO-941

MARRIED AND FREE

This is a very good book!
It's just such a tragedy
that so very few United Church
Pastors understand the need
for this personal relationship
with Jesus, that Gordon Hunter
talks about.

MARRIED AND FREE

Gordon C. Hunter

WELCH PUBLISHING COMPANY INC.
Burlington, Ontario, Canada

Scripture quotations in *Married and Free* are taken from the Revised Standard Version of the Holy Bible unless otherwise indicated.

ISBN: 0-919649-68-8

© 1983 by Gordon C. Hunter

Welch Publishing Company Inc.
960 Gateway
Burlington, Ontario
L7L 5K7 Canada

All rights reserved. No part of this publication may be reproduced, stored in a retrieval system, or transmitted in any form or by any means without prior permission of the copyright owner.

Printed in Canada

CONTENTS

O magnify the Lord with me
and let us exalt his name together.

Psalm 34:3

THIS BOOK IS DEDICATED TO

John, Jane, Stanley, Marjorie and Angela —

five beautiful people who have given to
Anna and myself the privilege of being
their parents.

FOREWORD

I am glad to have the first word in my husband's writing on marriage. As you will see, it is not a manual on the subject but a collection of discoveries along the way. His illustrations are drawn from life and experience in more than 35 years of Christian ministry and 36 years of marriage.

A friend once said, "Gordon, do the thing you do best. Bring inspiration and encouragement to people." He has done that in this book.

Our lives are always in the making, and if we waited for perfection before writing these thoughts, would the manuscript have ever been completed? We are constantly changing while growing toward wholeness.

I see each of Gordon's books as expressing his life goals. Early in our courtship he said to me, "There are just two things I want in life—to serve our Lord and to marry you!" Years later we were at a banquet where he was to speak. I knew he was feeling a little down that night (unusual for him) and although I was sitting at the far end of the head table I wrote on a scrap of paper from my purse, folded and passed it to him along the line. It simply said, "I love you . . . Jesus Is Lord!" Later he remarked that it not only gave him the needed boost at the moment but reminded him of his words of so many years before. He has kept and treasured that bit of paper because of its double affirmation re his personal life and his work.

The more this book progressed the freer, through God's grace, we have become. We have learned, with changed attitudes and with practise, to be "slow to chide and swift to bless" rather than the other way around.

We like the words of the hymn sung at our wedding:

New every morning is the love
Our wakening and uprising prove,
Through sleep and darkness safely brought,
Restored to life, and power and thought.
If in our daily course our mind
Be set to hallow all we find,
New treasures still, of countless price,
God will provide for sacrifice.

John Keble

Gordon's acceptance and encouragement of the use of my talents extends my sense of usefulness and freedom.

May these pages bring hope and joy to you.

Anna Hunter

INTRODUCTION

"Darling, I want my freedom," said a young woman to her not-too-amazed husband. She had found marriage to be restricting, confining, suffocating. She felt trapped. She demanded space, air, liberation. She just wanted out!

Many marrieds feel the same way. Some have long since concluded that, in the light of today's mix of alternative lifestyles, the old-fashioned idea of two people committing themselves to each other for an entire lifetime is a sick joke, a form of slavery, and intolerable. How can two changing people declare to a changing world that they'll forever be a couple?

This attitude is not new. Irish-born playwright George Farquhar (1678-1707) said, "Marriage and hanging go together." The English dramatist William Congreve (1670-1729) agreed with him and stated: "Every man plays the fool once in his life but to marry is playing the fool all of one's life."

Cynicism is contagious, and many young couples choose not to marry because they don't believe they can make it succeed. Why take the chance? "Shacking up," as it is popularly called, seems to be the perfect answer—intimacy with freedom to call it quits at a moment's notice.

But this has its problems, too. As one young person expressed it, "If we'd been married we would have put forth a more genuine effort to make a go of our relationship and I'm sure we could have made it successful—and happy!" For every person who refuses marriage on the basis that it might "threaten my individuality" there are scores who have discovered that vulnerability is the name of the game, that there are deep values in marriage not realizable in cohabitation and that real love delights to move forward toward total commitment. So while one girl argued, "Let's not get married lest it spoil our love," another said to her live-in boyfriend, "If you really loved me you would ask me to marry you."

The '60s brought the sexual revolution, the age of permissiveness and the "new morality." Youth went on the march rebelling against many institutions, including marriage. Their watchword: "Whatever the institution is for, we're against." People were shouting for liberation, and against Puritanism and the Victorian mind-set.

But freedom hasn't materialized. Dr. Bruno Bettleheim, professor of educational psychology at the University of Chicago said, "There are just as many sexual problems now as there were in the Victorian age — maybe more." What went wrong?

The '70s brought disillusionment. People who had said, "Marriage as an institution is an unnecessary formality, a useless and outmoded piece of paper, discovered that sex outside the context of marriage can be a desperately lonely affair. They found out the hard way that what seemed only a simple matter of moving in together did not give security and that sex, being both free and easy, did not naturally lead to true companionship. People learned that in grasping for immediate satisfactions, the deeper joys of partnership in an enterprise bigger than either party eluded them.

In the '60s and '70s we grew accustomed to hearing phrases such as "anything goes," "no censorship," "do your own thing," and "let it all hang out." Then came the movie *Looking for Mr. Goodbar* in which the chief actress was a respectable schoolteacher by day, but somewhat of an alley-cat at night, frequenting the sleezy bars, forever looking for "the right guy." Her adventures seemed to typify the age. She became victimized by the very environment in which she sought her freedom. She was murdered. Was this movie trying to say something to our generation?

Real freedom demands control. Barbara Seaman, author of *Free and Female*, talks about the backlash against the casual sex in which many people are hurt. "It was as if there was a train gradually carrying us away from Victorian morality, but then the train became a runaway and a lot of passengers were injured. Now the brakes are starting to be repaired."

It is interesting that the major opponents of the Playboy philosophy are not the moralists but the feminists. They have marched, rallied, and picketed, saying to the world, "We've been had. We've been used and exploited by the pornography trade. We demand it be stopped!"

Sex merely for pleasure doesn't automatically bring pleasure. There's something within us that rises up and insists on something better, more satisfying. We are learning that freedom requires obedience to higher laws. Wanting freedom without boundaries or standards is an invitation to chaos. Every game of sport has its rules. Every artist must work within the necessary disciplines. A river without banks is a swamp. So sex under love's bonding in Christian marriage serves to set both partners free.

Freedom also requires ideals. Our nature is to strive, to reach for what is better with our heart set on what is best. There is no marriage, no matter how healthy, in which both parties, if honest, could not see plenty of room for improvement. Perhaps we should hear the time-tested words of Goethe (1749-1842), "Like everything else that is not the involuntary result of fleeting emotion but the creation of time and will, any marriage, happy or unhappy, is infinitely more interesting and significant than any romance, however passionate."

As in our individual lives we set up our heroes, so in marriage we drool over "the ideal couple." And many young people who have had it with trial marriage, shacking up, and no-fault, non-commitment living together, still yearn for that day when they can "get married, settle down and have kids." At one time they might have thought it was nice not to have to report to anyone or to account for the time not at home. But now they are quick to say that it's wonderful to know he'll always be there, or that I can count on her. So they have a new image of the ideal partnership in terms of life-commitment and security, and they dream of it going on and on, even into blissful eternity.

With freedom there comes self-esteem and fulfillment. Can we find it? I believe we can. And that is what this book is all about.

I CHOOSE YOU

"Yes, you did!"

"I did not!"

"But I distinctly heard you . . ."

"You think you heard me. You always take the wrong meaning from everything I say."

"Are you trying to tell me I'm stupid?"

"I didn't say that and you've never heard me use . . ."

"But . . ."

"Listen, why are we quarreling like this?"

"I don't know but sometimes I wonder why you ever wanted me in the first place."

"But honey, *I chose you!*"

That did it! Just three little words. Said purposefully and with a sense of pride they can restore calm and perspective, while communicating the deeper message, "I made a good choice back then and you'll always be my bride."

Irrevocable choice puts a kind of halo of worth around the head of our loved one. A father and daughter were having serious conversation. Life had been going hard for her lately and she was now in the painful struggle of rethinking her whole life meaning and goal. Finally he turned and asked point blank, "What is it you really want in life?"

Slowly lifting her chin from her fist a light began to glimmer in her droopy eyes as she replied, "I suppose the thing I want most is to have a man who will always treat me as his precious gem."

Chosen, guarded, protected, cherished, given a mantle of respect and a crown of creative expectation—isn't this what truly liberates the spirit? Mature lovers have a variety of ways of saying, "There's no one in the world quite like you," meaning, "I accept everything about you, good, bad and indifferent, even though at times

1

this may call for a good deal of patience."

This is realism—admitting imperfection, weakness and failure, but also affirming the process of change, of becoming, understanding that God is not finished with either person yet and that each is in the making still.

Taking pride in a choice we have made in the past suggests re-affirmation for the present. "I chose you. I knew what I was doing. I could see no one else. You were my one thought by night and day." All of that sounds very nice, but what about today? After years of strain and struggle, working out differences and disagreements, and holding the finer shades of our different personalities in dynamic tension, a couple may ask, "Where are we now?".

Remembering "I chose you," and going on to say, "I choose you," brings a present freshness into a marriage that keeps the relationship alive and growing. One day a couple asked for an interview and they insisted on a morning appointment. This puzzled me until I learned that this was their tenth wedding anniversary and they wanted to re-state their vows. So we went into our small chapel and in the presence of their two children, went through the wedding service step by step, phrase by phrase. Somehow hearing a couple pledge their faith and love to each other after ten years put a depth to the meanings of those words I had never felt before. They wanted to re-affirm their choice, renew their vows and make a fresh start.

This takes marriage out of the category of something that happened just accidentally with the negativism that questions, "How did I ever get stuck with you?" It takes out of marriage that fatiguing sigh which indirectly says, "This arrangement makes intolerable demands on me, interfering with my private ambitions and goals; but I suppose there's no way out!" It embraces marriage as a training ground for maturity which it surely becomes when two people continue in the painful process of changing and struggling with rejection, those feelings of being unappreciated and put-down.

To say, "I chose you," activates the will to override the circumstances and feelings of the moment. It also says, "I know that you and I are both changing, but I choose you even if you never change. I release you to be yourself."

All of this strikes at the root cause of a good deal of inevitable tension in marriage. Most marriages exist with a kind of conditional clause, unwritten but subtly felt: "I love you but I wish you would . . ." or "I accept you but when are you going to . . .?" We would like to remold our partner and somehow make him or her conform to our image of what we think they should be and do. This builds up pressure until the lid blows, angry feelings erupt and tempers fly. This, in turn, is sure to kill spontaneity and drown enthusiasm.

Marriage that is freeing says, "I choose you—warts and all! I choose to be your lover, the supplier of your deepest and most personal needs and am ready to take whatever risks may be involved. I expect to be hurt at times because this is an unavoidable part of the game."

Sometime ago I heard of a parachute jumper who landed, seemingly without trouble, in an open field. Before he could unbuckle his gear, however, a strong wind caught the downed parachute and began dragging him over the rough ground. He managed to scramble to his feet and tried to run but tripped in the tangled mess of ropes and attachments. Pulled across the road and through a fence, he landed in a gravel pit. Finally he got himself free but not until he had been battered and bruised, blood oozing through his ripped clothing. Later someone asked, "Do you plan to jump again?" and he replied, "Of course I do. This is what I volunteered for!"

The hazards go with the job and it is not different with marriage. Wedded bliss is not just a series of whims or a string of comfortable pleasantries, but times of hurt, misunderstanding and rejection, followed by renewal, re-affirmation and recovery.

The words of the marriage service are not, "Do you love?" but "*Will* you love?" This calls for intentional choice, a choice which is releasing because it sets no limits on what a loved one may become. It says, "I set you free to grow, to become all that is possible for you." This requires trust because there is always the possibility that the one you set free will grow away from you or beyond you, giving rise to the fear that if you don't hold on for dear life you'll be passed by, rejected.

I learned this the hard way. My wife, Anna, is an artist. She's always had this beautiful creative ability to see things in their potential and to make use of the most ordinary bits and pieces of things to make something attractive. My first gift, just weeks after we met, was a box of chocolates, something she wasn't supposed to have in the first place because she was very ill and in bed with rheumatic fever. However, other members of her family got into the chocolates while she took the tiny brown wrappers and made paper butterflies which she arranged on a kind of mobile over her bed. I was greatly impressed by this, and her special gift of creativity amazes me more as the years go by.

But our first years of ministry together took on a kind of rigid conformity. For me the church, with its demands, meetings, long hours and deadlines always came first. Then came the family—and we had five children. Anna sure had her work cut out for her, but what about her artistic gifts? Well, only if there was time, and there wasn't much. Even though she studied art and had produced many lovely pieces, there just weren't enough hours to let her creative imagination go free. Too many other things took top priority. Tomorrow was the day I would stay home so she could get away and be herself. But that tomorrow didn't arrive.

That is, until our seventeenth year of marriage! One Sunday I returned from the evening service to find her not at home. In my surprise I questioned the children. One replied, "Oh, she went out awhile ago and said she was going to church."

Church! She certainly wasn't at our church. Where could she have gone, and why? I sat down. Then I began pacing the floor, went to the kitchen for a snack, then to the front door for any signs of her returning. No sign. Finally she came in. What? Who? Where? Why? How could you? Full of questions, I gained little satisfaction from her begrudged answers. But finally my worst thoughts were confirmed— she'd been to a neighborhood church for a special lecture.

Resentment boiled in me. In seventeen years we had settled many kinds of issues but never anything like this. How was I going to deal with it? I was jealous and fearful. Was this the beginning of a trend? Was she planning to go there every Sunday night from now on? If so, what would the people in our own congregation think of that? And anyway, what was wrong with my sermons? I could see my entire ministry beginning to collapse.

Fully two days later I began to gain some perspective, and then only after we had dared to open up a whole kettle of other things that had been brewing for a long time. The basic issue was not her going to another church but her inner desire to find some expression for this long-neglected artistic impulse. She was beginning to assert herself. Yes, she was the minister's wife. Yes, she was the mother of five. Yes, she was nurse, cook, gardener, housekeeper, family counsellor and much more. But she was also a person in her own right. She was standing up to be counted. A larger self was beginning to stir and arise in her.

Reluctantly I began to see my part in all this. How could I have been so blind? So selfish? I had presumed on her position, taken for granted that she would always remain the same, and been insensitive

4

to the unfulfilled inner person. So through a good deal of heart-searching I wrestled with what it would require of me to set her free.

I'm not sure our conversation in this area is finished yet, even after thirty-six years. But at least something was begun then that made a distinctive difference in both our marriage and our ministry. Anna has gone on to further study and further involvement with a much higher degree of productivity than would ever have been possible had she simply resigned herself to the helper role of "the minister's wife." And I admire her more because of it.

Love can be nurtured only in freedom. When each partner in a marriage is free to love or not to love, love blossoms in dynamic spontaneity. It moves from being a dull, static, endurance contest into an intentional adventure, a daily choice.

A couple, married eighteen years, looked back on a turning point in their relationship when the hostility drained away and was replaced with a new kind of listening to each other. He explains: "We did a lot of thinking and talking during this period. I remember at one point realizing that I was choosing to stay married. Before that, I might have stayed married because of the kids or my conscience. Now I realized I really wanted to be married to Bev. We now know that we've got a good thing going. We're free to be married. But that freedom can easily be lost if we stop working and learning. When you know that God loves you, it helps you love yourself. And when you love yourself, you can love somebody else.

"We'll stay married. It won't be because of the children (they'll be leaving home in a few years) and it won't be because of a legal document signed in a church. It won't be because of what family and friends might think. And it won't be because we can't each make it alone. We'll stay married because we don't have to. We're free to stay married. It's a choice we have made separately and together, for the reasons we have mentioned and for some we haven't thought of yet."

Christian marriage is an intentional community. First you decide to choose. Then you make the choice. Finally you stand by your choice, "For better or for worse . . . till death us do part."

This ensures a high level of enthusiasm in the marriage. Boredom has no place to take root in the excitement and the adventure of continual development and growth. Change brings challenge.

One person said, "I don't think there's any way one human being can satisfy the needs of another human being for fifty or sixty years. When you marry, you're making promises for a person, yourself in the future, who doesn't yet exist."

5

In contrast, here is a couple, friends of mine, interviewed on their thirtieth wedding anniversary. "Imagine being married to the same person for all that time!" someone said. "Isn't that rather inhibiting?"

The husband replied, "But she's not the same girl I married. Oh, one thing has not changed and that is her openness to life and her determination not to miss anything. She wants everything she can get from life and she wants to give everything she has. She has been stretching her mind and capacity since the day I met her. She always wants to learn more, to do more, to grow and change. And that's great because what I want in a wife is a real person, who has a life of her own."

Then she spoke up. "I guess the reason we've stayed together is that we have allowed each other to be separate persons. We have similar values and goals and share our Christian faith. But we respect and trust each other enough to allow one another to run on separate, though parallel, tracks."

I like that phrase. It speaks volumes. It's the kind of marriage I want to have. It arises from two free people saying to each other, "I choose you . . . to set you free."

Jesus said, "I choose you" (John 15:16). And He stuck by his choices even though at times His followers were dull and disloyal, faithless and unbelieving, childish and stubborn. Somehow they knew that in the context of his choosing they were set free to learn, to change, to become mature.

When a couple consciously choose each other again and again, their marriage begins to live, breathe and grow into a magnificence all its own. They experience the thrill of being married *and* free.

ON BEING REALLY CLOSE

When I first laid eyes on Anna something inside me went POW! She held me in fascination. She still does.

Just sex appeal? That may have been the starting point, but I wanted to know her history, thoughts, feelings, impulses and motivations. I wanted to know the inner person. The same search and discovery continues to this very day.

At the same time I felt there would eventually be an end to this search. I would have found out all there was to know and that would be that! But, as our relationship developed, I discovered that the more I knew of her the more there was to know and the more keenly I desired to know it. This could be called *the mystery of intimacy* or, less technically, getting really close. Our courtship theme song could have been, ''Getting To Know You.''

Then came another discovery! In the process of knowing her I was also coming to know myself in a new way. I was becoming a somebody to myself because I was important to her. In letting myself be known to her, I had found someone who wanted to understand and love me. This was both exhilarating and liberating. We were giving each other a most precious gift—ourselves. And we were enhancing each other with growing value and increasing wonder. Everything in me was toned up. I had sweet dreams at night, a song in the morning, zest in my work, appreciation for everything and love for everybody. The world was beautiful. It was marvelous!

In some real way we were supplying to each other one of personality's deepest needs: to know and to be known. It has been said, ''You can't be human alone.'' Our sense of self-worth depends a great deal on how we think others value us. Just as no one can see his own face except as reflected, so we value and love ourselves only in the reflection of how others affirm and love us.

In a marriage this cannot happen in an instant but is a slow,

7

step-by-step procedure of trusting each other in the context of being loved, wanted and cherished. Any doubts about what is happening will interrupt the process. Feelings may be hurt. We tend to withdraw if we sense we are being invaded, hurried or in any way used to the other person's advantage.

Couples who are in love and covenanted in marriage find nakedness both natural and affirming. But this cannot happen meaningfully at the beginning of a relationship, because clothes stand for the protection of our privacy, not merely physical but also psychological. As a couple begin their marriage, each feeling comfortably assured that he or she is valued infinitely higher than anyone else in the entire world, they have a normal desire to shed those clothes because they become a hindrance to more complete knowing. The real coverings, however, are the invisible ones around the inner person. Self-disclosure, or removing these protective concealments, can happen healthily only in an atmosphere of trusting love!

Because we desire to protect ourselves, nakedness and sex become delicate matters which many people find difficult to handle comfortably. Sex outside of the context of honest love and total commitment not only turns sour but tends to become positively destructive, making a person feel cheated. So much that was thought to be there in potential simply doesn't materialize. Entered into with high anticipation, it turns out to be a denial of worth. At the beginning it looked like deathless devotion but at the end it makes one feel like a soiled rag to be thrown away. Sweet love has turned into bitter lust.

The lie in pornography and permissiveness is the idea that sex by and for itself can create intimacy. The truth is that without honest love sex only alienates further and can lead to the sharpest kind of loneliness and eventually to despair. If repeated it may destroy the hope that any relationship can be real or that there is any answer for the feelings of personal isolation.

In the movie *Last Tango In Paris*, featuring a couple casually in and out of bed, the man dies and the woman exclaims, ''I didn't even know his name.'' Instant, impersonal sex is always possible, but what communication there is, is only genital. It is self-defeating and empties sex of its beauty and meaning, turning the very act itself into something repulsive. Intimacy, being really close, must have meaning, giving a sense of personal uniqueness in a permanent world which married people develop and is all their very own. But this requires time and a good deal of patient love.

Everyone wants to be loved. To be loved we must be known. To be known we must be willing to reveal. To reveal we must trust and to trust we must be confident of being loved. Love is never satisfied with less than the whole person.

Intimacy, however, always runs the risk of being betrayed. As children we would play a game requiring us to close our eyes and fall backward into the extended arms of someone else who was there to catch us (hopefully) before we hit the ground. Needless to say, this required a great deal of trust. Many could not do it at all and some would not even try. It all depended on how much trust we were willing to put in our friends who kept reassuring us that they would not let us down.

So in intimacy we must let ourselves "fall" into the hands of another person. We entrust our welfare, our happiness and our future into their care. Off must come the masks so they can see us as we truly are, warts and all! There can be no pretense and no defense. They must know the real self behind the public self as the mystery unfolds.

What if we are rejected or laughed at? What if the other person doesn't like what he sees? What if the appearance of affection turns out to be manipulation? What if the other person turns out to be a compulsive clinger—a "mummy's boy?" What if we become victimized by the other's buried hostility, stored-up anger, or some other neurotic need? People can hurt each other by sickening self-centredness, having a need to use someone else to feed an inner drive to dominate or control. It was said of a certain weak-kneed woman who married a strong-willed man, "Well, she'll have every comfort but she'll always have to be a yes-yes person."

Being exploited will result in a person's withdrawal and rejection of the marriage partner. Even more, such experiences can turn a person away from the exciting adventure of intimacy because, through bitter experience, they are convinced it will never work. They believe that nobody can be trusted, that everybody is out only for their own good, resulting in the determined attitude, "I'll never be so foolish again."

But what's the alternative? Loneliness! Living in the fear of being really known, yet torn between that and wanting desperately to be known, all the time hoping that somehow, somewhere, somebody out there may still want to know, affirm and love us.

A cartoon shows a husband and wife preparing for bed. Turning to her he says, "What are you putting on? Not one of those cast-iron nightgowns? You used to wear flimsy, slinky gowns when we were first married!"

Whereupon she replies, "I didn't get cold then." Someone has defined loneliness as waking up at two a.m. and realizing that no one understands you, your goals or desires.

Everyone wants to "move in from the cold." Although we should be prepared for possible hurt because intimacy is a rocky road, full of potholes, detours and unforeseen dangers, the joys far outweigh the bruises along the way. There is increased freedom in learning to trust one another in order to be really close.

Yet, many are still unwilling to take the risk. They may fear that in giving themselves away they may never get their real identity back again. Lost forever under somebody else's control, they may think they have surrendered their separateness as a unique individual. Intimacy, in their minds, is suffocating and limiting, and memories of past hurts only serve to make them doubly cautious about letting themselves go.

A woman whose marriage had just broken up said, "I don't ever again want to be in a position where I can be hurt." If she holds to that she will be able neither to love nor to be loved because this possibility is the price of intimacy in a meaningful relationship that is discovering what it means to be free.

Must it be hurtful? No. Healthy intimacy is not suffocating, limiting or repressive. Anna and I can testify that learning to be really close can be liberating and fulfilling, an open avenue for exploring and finding more in one another. We have released each other to go separately along the paths of our individual interests in reading and self-expression, yet have been sensitively aware of each other's thoughts and feelings along the way. There has to be breathing space in intimacy or growth is hindered. We have found freedom to give this to each other because of our deep commitment to be faithful and continue to nourish our marriage.

Couples who are really close in this sense can be together even when they are apart. They are interested in each other's private worlds, though not involved, and are present to each other without necessarily being engaged in the same activity at the same time.

When I am away from home I find myself thinking Anna's thoughts or imagining what they might be. When talking with someone, while expressing my own opinion, I unconsciously ask myself what she might say in the situation. If I read something exciting I mark it so I can share it with her on my return home. In a cafeteria line I tend to pick the foods I think she would choose, eating more of her favourite cottage cheese than I would when at home. Occasionally I may even go so far as to choose liver! Why is it that often when she is away, though I may sleep soundly, I wake up on her side of the bed and on her pillow?

Through intimacy marriage partners have the key to enhancing their sexual uniqueness as male and female. In this respect we can either feed or starve each other because only a husband can make his wife truly "feel like a woman," and vice versa. If and when this may be denied, uncertainty and frustration tend to take over. Troubled marriages are hungry marriages, hungry for those affirmations that intensify the sense of being a man or a woman.

Intimacy also contributes to a woman's beauty and a man's good looks. A man sees his bride as being very beautiful, but through the years of intimacy he will love loveliness into her. She, in turn, will make his features more attractive. In fact, we are told that couples who are deeply in love tend to look more and more alike as the years come and go.

The hunger for ever greater intimacy is perhaps never totally satisfied but becomes a wonderful cycle of on-going adventure and discovery. The more you have, the more you want, and when more is given, more is returned.

Even in the best of marriages, however, there are times when intimacy seems violated. Taking too much for granted, we may allow other responsibilities to crowd in, and then unintentionally begin to neglect each other. Or, we may not care to make the effort to understand, to be tender or patient. The important thing is not to be afraid to express our true feelings, accepting them as part of the tussle of living out our lives together on a daily basis. If we are senstitive and willing to say quickly, "I'm sorry," these negative feelings need not pose a threat nor undermine our permanent commitment to one another.

As mentioned in the last chapter, Anna is an artist with a beautiful, God-given talent to "speak the unspeakable" on canvas and through design. I am growing to appreciate that world but do not fully share it. Yet when she is in her studio, part of me is there, too, wanting to encourage and affirm her in whatever she may be doing. Occasionally I make stupid remarks that only reveal my ignorance and which she graciously overlooks. The important thing is that we are present to each other without being physically at each other's side or in the other's way. This is being close.

We often quote to each other the words, "Love is always eager to believe the best" (I Corinthians 13:7, Moffat's translation). We find this a refreshing note which helps us to restore intimacy in the face of possible misunderstanding. It means that if I truly love her, I will not lose faith but take her at her best and interpret what she may say or do in the best possible light. I will give her the benefit of the doubt and refuse the temptation to be suspicious or jealous or judgmental. This is a key that unlocks many otherwise closed doors to intimacy. It leads to restored communication and a fresh listening to one another in renewed love.

One of the most subtle hindrances to intimacy is holding secrets from one another. In our youth we needed a few secrets to break our emotional dependency on parents and to establish our individuality. In marriage, however, secrets become a barrier to honest, open communication. When the burden becomes too great husbands or wives may then seek out someone else who is willing to listen. Men may do it at the tavern, women over the bridge table, youth in a restaurant booth. This at least provides a temporary feeling of liberation. In some small way, by revealing our inner self we are looking for affirmation, while at the same time listening to other people's secrets and affirming them. It makes everybody feel better and builds up self-confidence.

Letting go of our secrets calls for selectivity. We don't share them with just anybody but only with those whom we trust, who will listen and understand without judging or telling others. If it is a guilty secret then we are relieved and liberated in the telling of it.

In my travels I frequently listen to people pour out their troubled feelings. At first this bothered me. In these situations I am a visitor, not a "father confessor." But one day it occurred to me that they probably seek me out for the very fact that I am not part of their regular fellowship or permanent community. I'm neutral. They can "spill it all" knowing that it will be held in confidence. They are relieved of the burden without having to reveal it to close associates. So the thing I had resisted has turned out to be an important and necessary ministry. It is a vital part of our becoming whole.

I have found that people want to tell all. For their own health and well-being they need to tell all. Call it confession or catharsis or just "unloading," we cannot bear our secrets. We want to be known, to come clean, to have it "up and out." People will pay large sums to professional counsellors and therapists just to have someone who will listen, to whom they can unburden themselves and be free.

We can only guess at the mountain of anguish that exists in our society. There is an inner world of fears, doubts, resentments and unhealed memories which cries out to be shared. From time to time these may erupt in a fit of temper, or a crying spell that is said to be "just nothing." Or it may show itself in physical symptoms such as allergies, headaches, ulcers or just plain fatigue.

Most couples in the early stages of marriage experience the joy of sharing secrets, finding it easy to say, "We'll be forever happy because we'll never hold anything from each other." Good for them. Before long, however, they may find themselves not saying all that they really feel so as not to hurt their partner, or to avoid a crisis, or perhaps just to save time. In order to preserve the euphoria of their love they innocently hold something back, thus creating a secret world of thoughts and feelings. In this way a married couple who have enjoyed honest intimacy may become almost like strangers to each other. Unless dealt with early in the game this problem could build up until the whole situation seems hopeless, and one partner flees into the arms of somebody outside the marriage who is all too ready to give a sympathetic ear. This is the road to "the other woman," or to that "harmless relationship." In such a situation sex may play no part, but it wasn't sex that was wanted in the first place; the need was for someone to listen and understand.

Some couples, rather than seeking out a counsellor or friend, decide to just "ride out the storm." But the storms tend to become more frequent, each lasting longer than the one before. They may then begin to regard their condition as normal, adapt to conflict as a lifestyle and settle in to live in perpetual competition with each other. One man asked, "Why does my wife always have to take the other side, no matter what I say?" Each had been playing the game of one-upmanship in a vain attempt to hold personality intact.

The good news is that things don't have to take that turn. Closeness can be re-established when a couple are willing to confess to one another and to forgive. If I withhold a confession from Anna it is often because I fear she will not confess her own part in the incident. I am longing to say those two most difficult words, "I'm sorry," but I wish she would do it first. How silly this is because, as invariably happens, when I do take the lead in confessing she quickly admits her contribution to the whole mess and says so. Soon we are in each other's arms and/or on our knees asking God to forgive us both.

When the vicious circle of emotional starvation is finally broken and the compounding cycle of mutual accusation is ended at last, the joy of homecoming is incredible. We reopen the doors to our inner selves, rediscover each other and re-establish intimacy. This is at the same time the most difficult and the most rewarding experience. We have to let go of our pride, break through the wall of hostility and become vulnerable to each other once again. Each time a couple go through this process it might seem their relationship is on the brink of disaster, yet this is not true so long as they are willing to give up hidden secrets and remember that true love, after all, is unconditional.

It is important at these times to become aware of what is really going on, what factors led up to it, what attitudes contributed to the breakdown of intimacy. Then the evident issues may be seen to be not the real ones at all. Rather, these lie beneath a mound of superficial matters.

It has been said, "The only real mistake is the one from which we learn nothing." I agree. If we can sort out within ourselves what the true aggravation was, or is, then we are ahead. We can ask ourselves, "Do we really want to continue in this victimized state of self-defeat? Have we known joys of intimacy so that we long for a return?" We may conclude that we've paid too great a price for our pride and most of the issues that divided us were not worth either the time or the energy we paid out.

Since we have entered the latter half of life and marriage, Anna and I are realizing more each day the *preciousness of our time together*. Quarrels that could leave us frustrated, tired and behind in our daily work are just not worth it. Life is too short and our joy in being close is too great so that to miss one single day of it would seem nothing less than a crime.

On one occasion when a sharp difference had come between us, I remember thinking, "I haven't time to deal with this now (I was preparing a lecture to be given that same evening) but I'll sure get even with her tomorrow!" But the next day I could not, for the life of me, recall what the issue was or what I wanted to say or what led up to it. Now I was angry with myself for losing my ammunition. On more careful reflection, however, I began to see that as a good sign, an indication of a little more maturity. I concluded that when you can't remember what the quarrel was about, things are more or less in proper proportion and the whole issue wasn't that important anyway.

These words were on a poster: "Sometimes we talk for hours and never say a word." Intimacy doesn't require words, in fact, talking often gets in the way. True dialogue goes beyond words, and silence can often enhance the meeting of heart with heart in tenderness, understanding and total acceptance.

14

How does this come about? Well, if there are no hidden secrets there is no need for cheap talk or for chit-chat about a hundred minor things that have little or no consequence. There is no resentment boiling under the surface or competitiveness looking for ways to take advantage or put the other in the wrong. This kind of relaxed quiet is not a heavy silence but light and easy and productive. It is conducive to ''the peace that passes all understanding'' (Philippians 4:7). Nor is it empty but full to the brim with all the important things we want to say and hear. Comfortable silence has no fear. ''There is no fear in love'' (I John 4:18). It is free from threat because it is full of trust.

It is in such an atmosphere of restful silence that Anna and I have found we can be most creative. If I am not spiritually and emotionally close to her my springs of creativity dry up, my thoughts are jumbled and I begin fighting within myself for ideas. What must it do to the creative person in her?

Silent times are conducive to in-depth listening, with the ears of the heart. I can guess what my wife is feeling by the way she walks across the room or picks up a paper or sets a table or does any little thing. And she may tell the same of me. Does this mean we can ''read each other like a book''? No, for that would make persons into objects. In intimate silence we can read each other's feelings and thoughts and even share meaningful dialogue.

We can only know as much of ourselves as we are willing to confide in each other. If I sense a boundary around something Anna wants to keep from me I may react with fear, cutting off some portions of myself from her in subconscious retaliation. But if I react with love and patience, the barrier comes down and I am invited into her confidence once more. All of this can take place in the silence. It is far more than body language. It is language of the soul. It is being really close.

IS EVERYBODY LONELY?

Tom and Joan were scurrying away from the insular community in western Canada where they had been brought up. In a little red sports car they crossed the Rocky Mountains, ''ate up'' the Prairies and the forests of northern Ontario, and finally arrived in the big city of Toronto. They were soon engulfed in its enormity and it scared them. But before long they both had jobs and everything began to look rosy.

Tom tells it. ''We imagined we were skating on a limitless lake with the wind at our backs and all the time in the world. Then the ice gave way and we were plunged into the stone-cold, bottomless city and we panicked, trying to breathe, trying to stay afloat, trying to keep our last precious warmth.''

Up to this time they were held together by coincidence and shared feelings of affection and adventure. But now they felt an urgent need to cling together to brave the hostilities of urban life, so they decided to get married.

This move turned out to be the beginning of the end. Tom says that like that little red sports car that brought them east, their marriage had no troubles on the downhills and did pretty well on the level, almost flying at times. But uphill was another story. They tried. They struggled. They ''coughed'' and ''spit'' and ''chugged.''Two years and several apartments later Joan moved out.

''When it comes to falling in love,'' says Tom, ''I'm a champ. I can do it on an elevator or waiting for a traffic light. I'm pretty good at being in love; the sensation of feeling the universe redefined is heady stuff. But when it comes to loving, I think I should be rigged out with a bell and a sign that says, 'unclean.' I suspect that through love I am looking for some way to love myself and that is next to impossible. And this is a terrible reason for loving someone else. Lovers end up as victims.''

17

"Our marriage," he continues, "had no natural momentum beyond panicky need." He concludes," The only sensible, emotionally sound way to live is alone. I realize now that living with someone and loving her is the hardest thing I can imagine doing. WE HAVE TO FIND A WHOLE NEW WAY OR WE WILL BE ALONE FOREVER."

The horror of being alone, perhaps forever—is this what we are all trying to run away from? A psychologist says, "In order not to be lonely, people will do almost anything—go broke, tell lies, steal or engage in sex."[3]

A Hollywood movie starlet said, "After working all day I must have a man to share my bed with me at night because the night can be long and lonely without a man. I've gone on with dead relationships for as long as a year out of pure fear, the fear of not being loved by anyone, the fear of final loneliness."[4]

And yet, as most couples will testify, marriage can bring its own peculiar kind of loneliness. "The loneliest people in the world are married couples living under the same roof who can't communicate," says one observer. Many of these people entered marriage with the starry-eyed idea it could be the end of all their problems, only to find themselves thoroughly disillusioned and looking to divorce as the one ray of hope to end the nightmare. Higher expectations only result in deeper hurt. Greater trust brings sharper grief. More self-giving brings more certain rejection, and the brighter the hope for recovery the deeper the despondency when it doesn't happen.

So while there are many today who make light of marriage, many others expect far too much of it. Like a set of pulleys designed and guaranteed to bear the strain of five hundred pounds, they want it to lift a ton. The marriage begins to reel under too much stress. Then the magic fades, the glow disappears and the loneliness is more painful than ever because now it is mixed with a sense of failure, futility and defeat.

Human loneliness is deeper than any one person or group of people can overcome. It is not a matter of simply being alone. "I've spent many a day alone but never a lonely day," a friend of mine said. Many who are constantly in the presence of other people are still profoundly lonely. Professional, syndicated help-givers sometimes counsel lonely people to join a club, begin a hobby, take a cruise or even join a church. But none of these ideas work very well because the advice is too shallow to cure such a deep malaise.

A psychologist identifies this kind of loneliness that gnaws at everyone as "existential loneliness." Another calls this "lonely loneliness." It arises from *angst,* the anxiety of being. It is the fear that the universe may be empty, that there is no ultimate Being who knows or cares, and that therefore there is no final meaning to anything.

This thought may be suppressed by prolonged work hours or frenzied activity or entertainment or pills or alcohol. But not for long. The sense of meaninglessness never completely goes away. It eats away at us like the gnawing of a mouse. It's like a dripping tap that drives us to distraction.

Mary and Joe were participating in a Marriage Enrichment weekend attended by a friend of mine. He told me how they felt so out of place. In a small group, Mary said, "You people all sound so happy in your marriages. But ours is . . ." She staggered into silence, then tried again. "Ours is . . ."

Tears came. They waited, frozen, her pain suddenly exposing the quivering anguish of others in the group. Word by word, she dragged her aching isolation out—all the way from her toenails, it seemed—and laid it before the rest. While the children were growing up, she and her husband had a common goal in which to submerge their differences. But now "Oh, the people in our community think I'm God's gift to organizations. They can always count on me for a job in the church, or the school, or Guides, or whatever. But I'm not doing it for them. It's for me. I need something—I'm desperate! At home I try to talk to my husband. I make him a special dinner; I sit down and give him a kiss or hug. And he turns on the TV. It's like he doesn't want me. I can't fight with the TV so I do things in the kitchen or clean up the basement. I really tear into it. I get all kinds of things done. . . but . . . but, . . . Oh, God."

Does marriage, even a fairly "normal" one automatically re-move loneliness? There is no guarantee of that. In fact the loneliness may be intensified.

It would appear that there is no way out of loneliness on the human level either in marriage or out of it. A professor at Oxford says: "This is more than the solitariness of a prison or the severed life of a woman deserted by her husband. It is more than the emptiness of one who is without friends. It exceeds by far the sense of failure in a hive of success. It is beyond the brave, smiling resignation of the person who spends life with memories. It is a darkness blacker than that which enshrouds the mentally ill. It is a sea more vast and threatening than that on which the grief-stricken are set abruptly adrift. It is a hopelessness with no horizon. It is a stifling cell whose walls and roof press ever inwards. It is the vast, empty, desolate territory of the ones who are adrift from God.'' [5]

For children, at least, freedom from loneliness is found in the security of home. On a beautiful June day our youngest girl Angela was happily skipping with her little friends. Marvelously complete, their world was filled with playful laughter and sounds of glee. Suddenly she slipped on the cement curb and came screaming into the house with blood running down her leg and dirt ground into the wound. In a split second her delightful world had crashed.

Anna ran out to investigate the trouble. Seeing the blood, she took her into the washroom and proceeded to clean up the wound, apply a bandaid and wipe away the tears. Angela, now comforted, began to gain some composure. Gently Anna led her to the front door and said she could go out again to play until she was called for supper. But Angela stood there without moving. ''Go on out,'' her mother said, ''your friends are waiting for you.'' But she refused to budge. With a mother's deep intuition Anna sensed what was needed, bent over, put her arms around Angela and gave her a tender, motherly hug. In a moment Angela broke free and scampered out to play.

Obviously the bandaid was not enough. She wanted a personal touch, the assurance of love higher and stronger than herself in order for her world to be pulled together.

Adults are much the same. We build our own play-world or work-world or marriage-world, all the time knowing in our bones that they are temporary. In a bad marriage where selfishness, moodiness and pent-up anger destroy communication, we at least have something to grapple with. Wise counselling, a good book on marriage, a listening friend, may help. Patience and compromise might soothe at least for a while. But what do you do with a good marriage in which two people long for richer fulfillment, hope to be together forever and feel that all eternity is not time enough for their love?

Could it be that loneliness is part of God's plan? If pain can be a good thing warning us of trouble, so loneliness could be a signpost pointing us to the only place it can be alleviated—to God Himself.

A woman found this to be true after surrendering her life to Christ. For long years she had been dissatisfied with life in general, full of fears, ineffective in her work and disillusioned with what she considered shallow friendships. One night in a meeting she said she felt tormented by ''a terrible cavity somewhere in the abdominal region.'' Being encouraged by loving friends, she did the very thing she had been resisting all her adult years—she turned herself over to God. Two months later she said, "The overwhelming emptiness has vanished and not come back." She had made the discovery that her inner loneliness was really a longing for a heavenly Father, someone to whom she could ultimately belong.

What might this mean in a marriage? Well, one writer says that we always marry the wrong person, meaning that the success of a marriage is not determined by our marrying the right person either by chance or choice. Two "wrong" persons, relating themselves and their marriage to God, can produce a "right" marriage.

For one thing, they find freedom from that gnawing sense of loneliness. Knowing God's love they are now better equipped to love each other. God, their divine companion, liberates them from neurotic dependency on one another. Having God as final truth they are no longer in bondage to the necessity of always having to speak or act as the ultimate authority. Finding security in God they can now take the risk of growth and change. They will also discover that their affection for each other can go deeper, even while holding opposite opinions on a great variety of subjects. They can be individually themselves. They are free to set each other free, to celebrate their marriage on a day-by-day basis.

For instance, Sandy says of her marriage to Jim, "It didn't have a chance in the world. Jim is a Jew who was bar mitzvahed when he was thirteen and I am a Gentile, confirmed in the Episcopal church when I was twelve. We met at college and were married shortly after graduation.

"I was bored and began to investigate Eastern religions, yoga, vegetarianism, white magic, witchcraft and even flying saucers—anything new and different. I was meditating, chanting, eating only the 'right' foods.

"Jim and I drifted apart and spent a good deal of time either fighting or ignoring each other. So we decided to travel. But while we hitchhiked we were no more than travelling partners. We had separate money, separate goals. And when we settled in a New England town we were just two roommates sharing the same house. We weren't sleeping in the same room; we weren't kissing; we didn't even talk except to argue. We had built up layers and layers of hatred so that our fights were unbelievably complicated and bitter.

"I lost interest in our home and stopped doing housework. Dirty dishes were piled in the sink. The house was a mess. We hated ourselves. Our marriage was gone and we were sick of soul. But for

21

all our seeking, we never had really been interested in God. We had only wanted to do things that were the latest spiritual fad.

"Then it hit us that the one thing we had never done together was pray. We hadn't thought of God as someone to pray to. He was just a feeling you have. We didn't know God was personal, that He loves us, that He longs to share the love of His Son with us.

"We picked up some scattered newspapers from the living room floor and knelt down—two dirty sinners—and began to pray: 'Our Father who art in heaven.' We prayed the Lord's Prayer over and over again, then we got up and cleaned the living room. We went to the bedroom and did the same. We spent the whole day kneeling down, praying and cleaning up.

"We knew then that God is a person. We had started that particular day hating each other. We couldn't talk; we couldn't even touch each other. But by the end of the day we were holding hands. It was a miracle. God had given us supernatural love for each other but then He also gave us back our natural love.

"The greatest thing we have learned about marriage in the past five years is that God is the only one who can make it work! He didn't pick two lovely, sweet people when He saved our marriage. He picked a couple of screaming bums. But Jesus came for sinners like us."

There is no one pattern for everybody. For many months after Anna and I were married I felt as if I were in heaven. Our marriage was nothing short of being perfect. Surely, we thought, no other couple had ever reached the heights of love and joy that we were experiencing. I suppose it was a case of worshipping the ground she walked on. It was pure ecstasy, at least for me, and anything more truly wonderful I could hardly have imagined.

Then a few things began to threaten our ivory tower existence. Differences and tensions came as if out of nowhere. Our humanness began to show and I was troubled. It was not so much the issues themselves that disturbed me as the fact that we should have any differences at all. I had much to learn.

Even in our happiest and freest moments I began to experience an inner fear, a kind of hesitation. Upon analysing this it dawned on me that this resulted from the haunting thought that our marriage couldn't last forever. Questions flooded my mind. What if she took ill? What if she were in an accident? What if something should happen that I couldn't handle? What if . . . ?

Then it dawned upon me that I had been bordering on idolatry, a denying of the very God whom we both felt had brought us together in the first place. I knew I needed to repent, to surrender our marriage to God. Then I could risk every day of life knowing that only God is worthy of our worship, of our total devotion, and that only He can remove our fear of what might happen, yes, even death itself.

When we surrendered our marriage to God there came a new peace which has remained with us through the years. The ecstasy and the joy returned but were now on a much firmer foundation. Our most comfortable, cozy, happy times now are when we experience the supportive strength of companionship, just being together, a mutuality of shared life that is surely a taste of what can be completed only beyond this world.

Furthermore, the dread that it will not last forever is gone. We can squeeze, laugh, kiss, pray, release. We are free to celebrate. The fact that it is temporary so far as this world is concerned only adds to the tenderness. And when she rubs my back, Wow! We have discovered "the sacrament of the present moment." It is a taste of eternity.

The only adequate answer to loneliness is fellowship with our Father God. In Him we are together forever.

SHOULD WE TELL ALL?

One morning Anna drove downtown. Toward late afternoon she returned having done all her errands and then cooked her usual delicious supper for the family. All was well until I went out of the door to attend a meeting and to my astonishment found no car in the driveway. Thinking that it may have been stolen, I rushed into the house.

"What's happened to the car?" I shouted. "Where is it? Who used it last? Where are the keys?"

Dead silence! Then Anna put her hand to her mouth and gasped, "Oh my goodness, I left it downtown!" Yes, it was true—she had come all the way home by subway and bus, and then walked several blocks, never once remembering the car!

Moments like these can make or break a marriage. I suppose some husbands would react by taking their wife in their arms and saying, "Oh you beautiful doll! You are so cute when you do stupid things." Not me! I couldn't rise to the occasion this time. In a moment I went through surprise, bewilderment, disappointment—with perhaps just a pinch of anger mixed in. Could such a thing really happen? Under my breath I asked, "How could you? What were you thinking of all the way home?" My beautiful wife just stood there in stunned yet dignified silence.

In the nick of time I stopped myself from exploiting the situation and taking advantage of her obvious embarrassment to vent several subconscious grievances I had been holding for some time.

"Have you never done anything like this?" she asked.

I couldn't remember anything at the moment so I quickly answered, "No!" In my inner self I knew it was a lie. Why had I reacted so vehemently? Earlier that morning, knowing she had a busy schedule downtown I had said, rather casually, "You should be leaving now."

This naturally rubbed her the wrong way and she replied, "You shouldn't use the word *should* because that implies blame or judgement.''

I really had not meant it that way but that's how she heard it. So I said nothing at the time and let it pass as just another one of those smallish incidents that take place in the daily banter of all married people. But I suppose it had been festering in my subconscious and now, when it seemed I had her cornered, it jumped out in a combination of ridicule (how could anybody be so absent-minded?) and blame (how will I get to my meeting on time?). Thanks to our daughter Marjorie, who volunteered to take the bus downtown to retrieve the car, I did get to my meeting, though, needless to say, somewhat later than I had planned.

I have discovered that whenever I criticize my wife it is almost always because there is something I am trying to suppress. The psychologist calls this "projection of guilt," using the other person as a scapegoat for our own failures.

It would seem that we all carry an unconscious burden of guilt, often not connected with anything we have done but just the result of what we are. The Bible says, "All have sinned" (Romans 3:23).

In his book *I'm O.K., You're O.K.*, Thomas Harris says that all infants are born with not-O.K. feelings. A psychologist writes: "The new school of Existential Psychology finds that there is one basic and ineradicable anxiety at the root of every human being, a normal, built-in fear, a sense of distortion, estrangement, homelessness or guilt, which seems to be a part of human nature."[6] The founder of the Club of Rome, Aurelio Peccei, contemplating our human condition, concludes that "There must be a deeply embedded flaw within us."[7]

If a stencil has a mistake, all the copies from the machine will carry that same flaw. But trying to correct every single sheet of paper means never catching up with the reproduction process. The only way to put it right is to correct the original. So with our human nature. Something very basic has to happen in what we are to make any real difference in what we do. Blaming others accomplishes nothing except inviting retaliation which results in even deeper misunderstanding.

Some people, on the other hand, take a morbid delight in doing just the opposite: that is, taking all the blame on themselves. They may even go so far as to condemn themselves for things they haven't done, thereby adopting a martyr complex. Policemen are aware of

26

this quirk in our nature. People will turn themselves in for crimes they have not committed, or they will commit a crime just for the sake of being punished, feeling they deserve it. A good example of this is found in Dostoevsky's novel *The Brothers Karamazov,* in which the father of the family is murdered by one of his many sons. Every brother at some time or another pleads guilty except the one who actually committed the crime.

A man was on trial for a felony. The jury found him not guilty. Immediately he began to fret, turned to brooding, quit eating, would speak to no one. Five days later he hanged himself.

An extreme case you say? Yes, but in the complexities of marriage who knows how many otherwise normal people set in motion a variety of ways of self-punishment: ulcers, allergies, migraine headaches and even more serious illnesses?

The fact is, there is no way we can rid ourselves of the guilt which one writer calls "the horror not to be borne."[8] Playing the game of "It's all your fault," or trying to even the score by saying "It's all my fault" only exaggerates the situation and drives us into deeper separation and misunderstanding.

Why is it so difficult for us to admit complicity in each other's failures and faults when, to a large extent, our mates become what we make them? Willingness to be open and understanding enables the other person to blossom and grow into fulfillment of personality. Conversely, if we are always on the defensive, interpreting otherwise well-meaning statements as criticism, we thereby cut ourselves off and break the fragile lines of good communication.

The fact is, we are defensive by nature. Even a child is quick to say "It's not my fault." Accepting blame only adds to the burden of unconscious guilt we all bear until it becomes intolerable. Criticism is destructive, in this sense, because it demeans people, puts them even further down in their own estimation and undermines their feelings of self-worth. Rejection, then, calls forth an even sharper response which, in turn, attacks the self-esteem of the first person. This can go on and on in a vicious circle until, as one woman put it, "We were re-enforcing each other's self-destructive tendencies." Married people thus undermine each other by harsh judgement or subtle ridicule.

Paul Tournier writes: "Any person under the rebuff of accusation has a defensive reflex of self-justification. A reply to the accusation immediately springs to mind. Arguments come flooding up, leaving no room for confession of his faults. He can offer a thousand good reasons to exculpate himself. He is accused of cowardice; every occasion on which he has shown courage crowds into his memory. He is accused of lying: the recollection of other people's lies comes to mind and he judges himself, on the contrary as being too frank; it is those who, by their unjust conduct towards him have caused him to lie who are really responsible.''[9]

To protect ourselves we may sometimes not criticize directly but withdraw within, making of ourselves a kind of protected castle with a high wall all around. If the other partner in the marriage does the same, we have two people under one roof living in almost complete isolation. This tragic state of affairs can continue almost indefinitely.

To be sure, in everyone's life there is a need for some privacy in which to blossom and grow. But secrecy is another matter. Secrecy involves keeping ourselves from being known by our mate, and if we are not willing to be known we cannot be really loved. "Getting to know you,'' and "getting to love you'' go hand in hand. Nor can our mate force his or her way over the walls of our self-made castle. They are insurmountable. Only as we ourselves are willing to bridge the moats and open the gates and welcome our mate in can we be known and genuinely loved. This is a risky business because of our fears that we might not be loved when we are totally known. In that case we keep pushing the other person away, relishing opportunities to catch our mate at fault or to exploit obvious imperfections, thereby bolstering our own defense.

A movie actor whose marriage had just "totalled'' said, "Each morning when I get up, I get dressed, and the last thing I put on before I go out is a rubber face, so I won't show what I'm feeling inside and be able to get through the day.''[10]

One night I sat in a group discussing marriage. Someone made the suggestion, which was generally accepted, that the time had come for contractual marriage, that is, marriage for an agreed-upon, limited number of years. When that term ended everything would be up for re-evaluation and another term could be undertaken providing it was acceptable to both parties. In a day of so many broken marriages this might seem like a sensible approach.

But when I asked the reason for this arrangement, one person replied, "So as not to feel guilty in making a promise that cannot be kept.'' "As long as we both shall live'' would seem to be too much to expect of frail human beings. Just make it ". . . as long as we both shall love.''

Many would allow similar concessions to human nature as the

28

only answer to the dilemma. A marriage counsellor says, "Whenever you give yourself completely to another person it ends up in disaster. Never give your whole self so that if they fail you do not collapse." He talks about a couple who tried total honesty only to find the relationship hopelessly doomed. "Openness, in this case, became a can of big, fat, wriggly worms," he wrote.[11]

Real love is not fully satisfied until it is all and forever, never contenting itself with limitation. A man put it, "My wife and I have learned to avoid subjects that produce friction. At the same time, some of my deepest feelings I am hesitant to share." A marriage cannot be comfortable and secure unless all areas are open for discussion and sharing.

Is there a way out of this dilemma? Can we somehow be rid of unconscious guilt, immune to the devastating effects of criticism and at the same time be open to admit our own failures and needs? Is there a more solid ground to stand on than human love alone, and is it possible to tell all, yet still be understood and accepted in love?

YES! God answers in Christ by way of the Cross. God comes to our rescue, freeing us from this trap of trying to protect our dignity and self-worth by our own inadequate techniques of dealing with our guilt. He makes Himself the scapegoat. He takes on Himself the burden of what we are as well as what we have done. If there is an inner integrity in every person that says "everything has to be paid for," He pays for it by His death on the Cross. The Bible says, "He bore our sins" (I Peter 2:24). It is His mighty love for us that leads Him to do this. We are worth that much to Him. By His grace the burden of our guilt and inferiority, our not O.K.-ness, is lifted. We know the privilege of being forgiven, not in any cheap way by His simply saying "forget it," but by His dying on the Cross.

Accepting this, we can have confidence and a sense of self-worth, not through accomplishment or performance, but because of our new-found freedom from the burden of guilt and its insidious consequences.

Now we can afford to be open, to be known, to confess our failures and to say, "I am sorry," without feeling that the whole structure of our inner being is about to collapse.

I watched an old dog lying in the sun directly under a birdfeeder. At first the birds kept their distance in the tree branches, their bird nature telling them to be wary. Would the dog suddenly jump up and grab? But he was deaf and oblivious to these creatures. After a long time one bird dared to come near, then another, and another, until all were feeding confidently.

So in marriage. When a couple find more solid ground to stand on than the frailty of their own defenses, they discover they can trust one another with thoughts and secrets which heretofore they had guarded with utmost care. They can relax their caution and be themselves. No longer afraid of being "found out," their marriage can breathe. They can laugh at themselves and each other without feeling threatened. As one man said, "There are just two reasons why our marriage isn't what it could be and I'm one of them." A healthy attitude!

And contagious also. The more we are willing to be honest with ourselves the more patient we are toward our mate and the more tender and understanding he or she is toward ourselves. Paul Tournier says, "Nothing is more contagious than confession."[12] A husband and wife with this attitude discover a new freedom to admit their individual needs. Such admissions are good therapy for body, mind and spirit. The Bible puts it succinctly: "Confess your sins to one another so that you will be healed" (James 5:16).

For one thing, the mask comes off. I watched a TV program depicting a clown putting on and then taking off a variety of masks, one happy, another angry and a third sad, et cetera. All the while his own face remained deadpan. Finally he put on a very funny face which brought forth much hearty laughter. Then it happened! When he tried to remove this mask, it would not peel. He pulled and struggled, attempting to get a hold on it from the bottom and then from the top. He tried twisting and then scraping. Nothing worked.

Gradually the message began to sink in. One sensed his terrible inner struggle to be rid of the false image. True, the mask was a very happy one, but it wasn't his true face. Behind this beaming facade was a despairing personality, saddled with the load of living a lie.

One man said, "The besetting torture of my life has been a sense of being in the wrong and liable to punishment. I have tried bluster, proclaiming that I was not in the wrong after all, and wishful thinking, pretending the haunting feeling wasn't really there. I've tried stern repression, resolving not to think of it. I've tried hard work, the pursuit of amusement and diversion, and God knows I've tried by getting drunk. Regardless of my evasive manoeuvers, there, when the chase was ended, it was—ready to pounce.

"It is hard for me to describe the terror that goes with this. I tense up and shorten my breath and feel scared. I go on the defensive at all points, fairly bristling, like a mental porcupine, yet with an underlying, deeply panicked sense that my defense is not going to be successful. It means ultimatums impossible to meet, ostracism and disgrace, an eternity of unfriendliness."

One night, in the presence of a friend, it all came out. His real self emerged. Through discovering God's love for him, made evident by the Cross, his real self was freed. He says, "The kindness of God and man made it possible for me to admit wrong. When I could admit it, I was spared the exhausting effort of trying to maintain the facade of phony bluster and pretense intended to conceal wrong. Though the experience is grueling, the reward is a life lived fully and actively before God and without fear."

Freedom! Indescribable freedom! When the masks come off, the true self can emerge.

Grounded in the unbreakable love of the eternal God, partners in a marriage are freed to know and be known. The barriers come down, fear of being exposed no longer exists, caution is thrown to the wind. Love can now flow—renewing, refreshing, re-creating love.

Little conflicts, annoyances and controversies are bound to arise but now a couple can know what to do with them, how to handle them, even using them as raw material for greater self-understanding and growth. Partners in such a marriage delight in granting each other privacy simply because there is no secrecy. They can dare to tell all because each has the confidence that the other has the desire to understand and forgive. Such a marriage moves forward into greater and greater freedom, and in that freedom is true and glorious fulfillment.

FREE TO BE FRIENDS

Sitting at breakfast one morning my eye fell on a cereal box bearing these words: FREE INSIDE. Applying this to marriage, I realized there can be no real freedom unless each partner is free inside.

A scene from the comic strip "Blondie" will illustrate what I mean. They are sitting in the living room, almost back to back—Dagwood absorbed in television and Blondie concentrating on her knitting.

Suddenly Dagwood turns in her general direction and says, "There was a ten-dollar bill missing from my wallet this morning."

Blondie replies, "It probably found a home in my purse."

"But, it already had a home in my wallet," says Dagwood.

Back came the answer, "Then let's just call it a home away from home." And with that Blondie assumes the matter is closed while Dagwood takes on a very puzzled look, wondering how to deal with a statement like that.

There's more here than meets the eye. Dagwood is free enough inside to bring a personal accusation, thus giving communication a chance. He might have led an attack by saying, "Are you the one who took . . .?" Or, "You had no business . . ." Or, "Can't a man even call his wallet his own?" Or, "You do this all the time." Or, "It was my last ten and I needed it today to . . ." Or, "You might have at least told me."

Any one of these would have thrown the fat into the fire. But approaching the subject obliquely, Dagwood merely reports a fact. We sense no emotional overtones, no ominous threat, no fear of consequences.

In the intimacy of marriage, almost any subject can lead to either fierce arguing or further conversation, depending on how it is hand-led. If a person is jealously guarding his rights, sensitive to any invasion of privacy, constantly looking out for ways to "catch" the other person in some misdeed, the marriage is snarled and the partners are caught in the entanglements of a win/lose situation.

Blondie is equally neutral in the situation. She simply says, "It probably found a home in my purse." Probably? This is an admission, but a very indirect one, because she knows that her husband knows where the money is and how it got there. It is as if she were saying, "If you don't blame me and I don't blame you, then let's blame the money itself." Because he is sufficiently free inside not to accuse her, he sets her free from the urge to defend herself or to react with anger.

If, on the other hand, Blondie were not free inside, she might have said, "What's wrong with you? You get so uptight about the slightest thing." Or, "How do you expect me to run this household on the pittance I get from you?" Or, "I thought from the time we got married that everything was 'ours,' including the money?" Or, she might have cut it off short by saying, "So? What are you going to do about it?" Some persons might have reacted, "Listen, I've had a rough day. Don't you jump down my throat or I'll give it to you right between the eyes." Here also is an opportunity to dig up a smelly bone of the past: "O.K., how about the time you . . .?"

Obviously Blondie is quite aware of the fact that it may not be entirely right to dig into a partner's wallet or purse. Still, life together presents the occasional circumstance which makes this kind of action necessary. An occasional invasion of privacy with confidence that our partner will understand indicates that marriage is on a firm foundation and the personalities free.

Further, in the running of this impersonal conversation we can detect a beautiful undertone of good humour. It's as if they are both saying: "This is life," "This is marriage," "This is wonderful." Humour is surely one of the most liberating agents available in a marriage. As long as a couple can laugh they are in control of the situation. When humour goes out, hurt or bitterness may come in.

A young couple were having a hard time financially while the husband finished university. They were barely making it on her meager income. One night she was typing his essay while he scrubbed the kitchen floor. Tired and discouraged, he was bemoaning their "crummy apartment." She turned to him with a smile and said, "Well, honey, things can't be all that bad so long as I have household help and you have a secretary."

They burst out laughing and felt released with a new perspective and new energy. They learned that you can live without something if you have something to live for.

Free inside! How can this be achieved? St. Paul says, "Love has good manners and does not pursue selfish advantage. It is not touchy. It does not compile statistics of evil or gloat over the wickedness of others" (I Corinthians 13:4-5).

Selfish advantage? A cartoon shows a woman pouring her husband's morning coffee. She had hurried out of bed, housecoat all ruffled, hair in curlers, eyes half-closed. Passing by a mirror she exclaimed, "Goodness, I'm a sight! I'm sure glad we're married!" Nobody needed to tell her; the mirror doesn't lie. Her remark was a joke, but it is no joke when we think we can get away with slovenly habits or an offensive disposition just because we're married. Love that is freeing is sensitive to the subtle ways we may be tempted to do that.

St. Paul describes a quality of relationship that reflects God's love for us. We cannot achieve it on our own but only as we desire to imitate that divine love.

Touchy? Compile statistics? Gloat over the wickedness of others? In marriage, only persons who are secure within themselves can respond sensitively to what the partner may say, do or think. There is no suspicion or fear that behind the words is some sinister plot to undermine or destroy one's self-confidence. There is no "hidden agenda" or battle strategy based on reciprocation or revenge. There is no desire to read the worst between the lines or to suspect motives.

Trustful love assumes that the partner is not out to gain some personal advantage. Competition quickly turns into co-operation. Picture a couple on a lake in a very leaky boat. One wants to start bailing while the other says their only hope is to row hard and make for the shore. Probably either method would work but not half and half. Both should bail or both should row. If there is basic distrust in the marriage they may start to argue, not about what to do but about whose idea is going to win out. Each may think that the other is just trying to prove him wrong or foolish. Unless this deadlock is broken the boat will go down and they with it.

If marriage goes, both individuals go, too. Both lose out. No one can win. In trustful love that is not trying to gain advantage, the assertion "I'm right and you're wrong" will seldom be voiced because no one is trying to defend himself.

A great breakthrough in liberating marriage comes when we

35

learn it is O.K. to be wrong, to admit failure, to say "I'm sorry" and be relaxed about it. Small-minded persons are forever defending themselves. To be centrally right and secure in a love bigger than momentary feelings can allow a person to be marginally wrong yet not turn to sulking with hurt pride.

Some people's vanity sticks out all over the place just waiting to be attacked. This makes them "touchy." Few things can boggle a marriage faster then this type of super-sensitivity. How do you handle this attitude? Do you ignore it, in which case communication tends to break down, or fight it so that someone's self-esteem is likely going to be beaten to a pulp? It's a no-win situation. Touchy people also have a way of collecting statistics on their partner concerning past mistakes or failures. They carry around "a gunnysack full of uglies," waiting to dump it at the appropriate moment. Some of this emotional garbage may go back for years and be concerned with things like "Why did you say what you did to my aunt at our wedding reception?"

But in a marriage that is truly free is there no place for a good fight once in a while? Of course there is. Persons who are free inside are also free to grapple with each other and still preserve the love-bond. Intimacy requires differences and occasional conflict to clear the air, to vent pent-up feelings and to express inner convictions. Couples who avoid having a fight for the sake of possible damage to their relationship are living with a fear which is like a ball and chain to a marriage. Moreover, they will probably adopt a "game plan" that could become a life stance such as always giving in and letting the other have his way, or refusing to talk because the other won't face up to tension. One man said, "Darling, let's not argue like this. Can't you see that it makes the dog nervous?"

A writer says we should learn to fight like a dog. One day while stopped at a light he observed a couple of dogs fighting. "It was fierce," he writes. "Then one chased the other across the street and it was over. Poof! Just like that. The victor trotted back smiling. The vanquished nonchalantly ambled down the street, stopping now and then to sniff the world.

"Dogs fight right. They're objective . . . fighting for food, females and turf. They don't try to finish each other. They use enough force to do the job, but no more. No overkill. When it's over, it's over—no pouting or resentment. Body damage? Some. Soul damage? None."[13]

Marriage that is on a sure foundation can risk conflict because, in the spirit of love, it can and will be resolved. However, there are good fights and bad fights. A good fight will deal with an issue as quickly as possible. St. Paul said, ''Be angry but do not sin; do not let the sun go down on your anger, and give no opportunity to the devil'' (Ephesians 4:26-27). Anger that leads to sin is anger that is not dealt with. Therefore it festers and grows and infects everything. Not to let the sun go down on our anger is to deal with it right away.

Sometimes this can be difficult. A famous television comedienne said that she and her husband never went to sleep until they settled all of their arguments. Then she admitted that sometimes they didn't go to bed for three or four days! Well, sometimes it may be next to impossible but it's a goal that should be upheld just the same.

A good fight will deal with one specific issue at a time. When a couple go at it ''hammer and tongs'' there is usually a lot of extra garbage that is dug up and thrown in at the same time; children, in-laws, work schedules, budgeting, and dozens of other matters can so clutter the scene that it becomes difficult to remember what the problem was in the first place. It all needs to be broken down into manageable hunks or chewable bites. Small success is better than the collapse of conversation altogether.

In a good fight a couple will make sure they talk *with* and not *at* each other. St. Paul said, ''Speak the truth in love'' (Ephesians 4:15). Someone has said that to speak the truth without love is brutality while to speak love without the truth is sentimentality. These two need each other to balance out constructive communication.

To be free is to be honest in expressing feelings whether they are good or bad. Only in this way can our individuality be preserved, emotions aired and ideas expressed. Otherwise one person or both are under oppression. Love needs fresh air in order to breathe. This can only come when a couple are open enough to be themselves to each other. Only then can each discover and explore the great caverns of understanding between them and come to say in the mystery of love and marriage, ''I love you as you are.''

Some couples stop before the fight is over, leaving the subject dangling in mid air and feelings still exposed and unhealed. This is damaging and unfair. Moreover, it is from the ground of unresolved conflict and unsettled issues that adultery often takes root and grows. Husband or wife or both seek condolence in the arms of some other person who will listen and sympathize. Most often it is not somebody else's body they desire but seek understanding and relief of loneliness. When two people meet on the basis of sharing their hurts in marriage they tend to quickly become more than "just friends" and find themselves sexually involved. Of course there is a lot of childishness in this, but in their determination to justify their position, they can be gradually drawn into this warm and inviting situation, remaining oblivious to what is actually happening and to the emotional hunger that is behind it all.

Unresolved conflict does not disappear but is expressed in some other way; husband or wife might take it out on each other or it may emerge in the form of a physicial illness or neurotic behavior. It may result in a person refusing close friendships, believing themselves to be incapable of a genuine relationship. Some people may become workaholics, leaving themselves no time to think. Unresolved conflict may change their whole view of life, the world and God into self-destructive cynicism. But none of this need take place at all if a couple are resolved to pursue their conflict to a positive, creative solution.

Nor is it fair to hit below the belt by exploiting each other's obvious weakness or by criticizing what is unchangeable. Ann Landers gives a list of never-to-be-used phrases in a family fight:

"I'm going to tell you something for your own good."

"I've put off mentioning this because I know how sensitive you are."

"I don't usually make comparisons, but my mother did it this way."

"I know you don't care much for my brother, but at least he would not have talked to his wife the way you talked to me last night."

In a marriage where two people are free inside, conflict will result in some creative conclusion or constructive proposal. Always the aim should be to end the argument in a clinch with the marriage not merely intact but actually stronger. If a couple trust each other's love this will happen without planning. A husband will not assume "She's out to get me," nor will a wife say to herself, "How can I beat him at

38

his own game?'' Rather conflict will provide rungs on the marital ladder to help a couple rise higher, understand themselves and each other more and have a greater perspective on life as a whole.

Some years ago Anna and I attended a wedding, a very beautiful occasion. The church was festooned with flowers, the bride and groom made a most handsome couple and all the guests were in their finery. In the midst of this exquisite setting the soloist, a charming young lady, sang, ''Don't Let This Moment Pass.'' It was a number I had never heard before, and it was so saturated with sentiment that before she was through practically everybody was reaching for kleenex.

Doubtless many thought it was wonderful but I felt it was a poor choice because it was literally asking the impossible. Right now I am sure that moment has passed just as it was meant to do. Not only did the wedding pass but the reception and the honeymoon went with it, and soon the bride and groom got down to the challenging but much less sentimental business of making a home and raising a family. Infatuation is fine but was never meant to last. The blind side of love that cannot see any defects in one's partner is sure to disappear, but this is in order that a stronger and more realistic type of love will take its place. To try to hang on to the immature love of a couple just starting down the marital road is sheer fantasy.

In contrast is the description of a recent movie as ''A LOVE STORY THAT BECAME A MARRIAGE THAT BECAME A LOVE STORY.'' That's marriage at its best. Nothing recreates love like having a new romance with the same person.

On the bureau in my bedroom is a motto which I look at frequently because it never fails to give me a lift: HAPPINESS IS BEING MARRIED TO MY BEST FRIEND. Sometimes lovers find it difficult to be good friends. They may be terrific in bed but have little to say to each other over a meal, still less in the living room where they may glue themselves to television as a means of relieving the tension of having to look at each other face to face. A well-known writer says, ''I know couples who are so well adjusted sexually that they've made a career of it; yet they can't have a piece of toast together without getting into a fight.''[14]

To be free is surely to be good friends, delighting in each other's company in any setting, learning to use crisis or conflict in ways that strengthen the bonds of togetherness. At the same time, good friends in a marriage are glad to give each other sufficient liberty to change and grow in order to fulfill their God-given potential.

The key to this freedom in friendship is to permit God's love to work through our human love. This divine love is clearly evident in Jesus Christ who said, "If the Son makes you free, you will be free indeed" (John 8:36).

SO MUCH MORE!

"Sex is beautiful, why spoil it by getting married?" This young woman was speaking for many for whom the whole thought of marriage has turned sour. Part of the reason for this may be the cynical attitude of married people themselves who thoughtlessly express to newlyweds their own inner disappointment by remarks such as "It isn't all it's cracked up to be." One man said, "Courtship is a very witty prologue to a very dull play." Another said, "The trouble with marriage is that it is so daily." Still another commented: "Before I got married I asked, 'How far can I go?' Now I keep saying, 'There has to be more than this.' "

Perhaps the greatest threat to many marriages is just sheer boredom.

Life goes on forever
Like the gnawing of a mouse . . .
And tomorrow and tomorrow and tomorrow
There's this little street and this little house.

Romance is gone, excitement evaporated, and the thrill of each other's presence just isn't there any more. What used to call forth enthusiasm has become tiresome. What once satisfied has now become a drag.

Boredom makes people tired, fed up with life in general and with marriage in particular. Trying to improve the situation seems futile. In a very stimulating book, *How Never To Be Tired*, Marie Beynon Ray says, "Boredom with housework has made women blind, boredom with a husband made them cripples, boredom with a mother-in-law has paralysed them."[15] In some young people it frequently leads to violence. Boredom lies behind many prison riots. A strike at an automobile assembly plant had as its central demand two more coffee

41

breaks—anything to reduce the boredom. Boredom admits that life has lost its meaning. The famous actor George Sanders, in spite of a very successful career, took his own life and left a note saying, "I'm leaving because I am bored."

If individuals can suffer from depression through boredom, so can a marriage. Wedded bliss turns into wedded blahs! A bored wife turns to her husband and says, "What do you want to do, Andy?"

He replies, "I dunno, Kit, what do you want do?"

To which she answers with a yawn, "I dunno, what do you want to do?"

This marriage is in a vacuum, having lost its inertia, its will, its motivation. It's hit the doldrums.

When I heard that a couple, good friends of ours, had decided to call it quits, I was shocked and dismayed. There was no previous indication that all was not well with their marriage, so one day I decided to come straight out and ask him what went wrong. His simple reply was revealing. "It just died," he said.

When one thinks, on the other hand, of what successful and happy marriage demands, it is astonishing that so many do survive and even thrive. Like the bumblebee, of which it has been scientifically proven that it can't fly, marriage often endures in spite of itself. Think of it—two human beings promising to share life together on all levels: physical, material, spiritual—a promise made in the face of all the uncertainties of the future. What can equal it for foolish gamble? If it does not last it will be because the partners have discovered something extra, not always immediately evident. They have more than just physical or emotional compatability.

The undeniable fact, too often ignored, is that we are made by God and for God. There is a God-shaped vacuum within us that only God can fill. We don't feel fully at home in this world. C.S. Lewis says, "If I find in myself a desire which no experience in this world can satisfy, the most probable explanation is that I was made for another world."[16] And again, "Our lifelong nostalgia, our longing to be reunited with something in the universe from which we now feel cut off, to be on the inside of some door which we have always seen from the outside, is no mere neurotic fancy, but the truest index of our real situation. We remain conscious of a desire which no natural happiness will satisfy."[17]

Lewis goes on to say that this longing for something beyond must be an indication that somewhere there is satisfaction. He says, "A man may love a woman and not win her; but it would be very odd if the phenomenon called 'falling in love' occurred in a sexless world.''[18]

Lewis also writes, "We are born helpless. As soon as we are fully conscious we discover loneliness. Our whole being by its very nature is one vast need; incomplete, preparatory, empty yet cluttered, crying out for Him who can untie things that are now knotted together and tie up things that are still dangling loose.''[19]

Moreover, Lewis makes clear, it is when we are happiest that we experience this inner longing the most. Joy emphasizes our pilgrim status; it always reminds, beckons, awakens desire. All our lifetime an unattainable ecstasy has hovered just beyond the grasp of consciousness.

Many others have expressed the same thought. An old song reflects it, "This world is not my home, I'm just a-passin' through." Or this verse by G.K. Chesterton:

> For men are homesick in their homes,
> And strangers under the sun,
> And they lay their heads in a foreign land
> Whenever the day is done.[20]

This longing for "the more" beyond that which we sense even in our times of greatest ecstasy is, then, a clue to the meaning of those experiences. They are guideposts.

In the light of this, sex becomes a pointer to something marvelously wonderful beyond itself, and is infinitely enhanced when that "beyond" is welcomed into the act itself. As one observer puts it: "It appears to me that bodies are not so much trapped in being body as they are feverishly trying to become spirit . . . and a person who experiences the profound nature of human and divine communion [finds that] mere genital sex is forever relativized and revealed for the avenue and window that it is. Such people will be capable of deeper and deeper communion and yet not likely enslaved to its momentary rituals . . . such is the positive character of human sexuality. Thus God has forever made human flesh the privileged place of the divine encounter.''[21]

When I was in high school I suppose I was just one of the boys who would gather in corners or in the snack shop to talk about the girls. We would joke and snicker and tell stories. But there was one particular girl who invariably came up in our banter about females in general. She had what we called "a reputation." It was whispered about her that she would let a boy "go all the way!" I think we held her in a mixture of awe, scorn and disbelief. Anyway, that little phrase, "all the way," held my imagination for some time. What must it be like to go the limit?

The problem with so many marrieds is that they don't go all the way. Some stop at genital sex. For them sex is purely a physical act which must always result in orgasm, hence they are preoccupied with gaining results in measurable terms. Also they look to better techniques, read sex manuals, try to keep up with the latest sensational revelation about "secret erogenous zones," and regard the sex therapist as the high priest of personal fulfillment. Such preoccupation only keeps them from the deeper experience of self-giving and the resulting self-discovery. They have deified the physical side only and their god has let them down. They have their fill and have nowhere else to turn. Their so-called heaven becomes hell because they feel exploited, used, disappointed. What began with great promise ends up in deep frustration. French theologian Jacques Ellul tells about sexual life which is "barren, a source of keen discouragement, and finally a search for more elaborate sexual techniques to make up for the emptiness of the meaning through the aggravation of the act."[22]

Of course, if we were just animals, genital sex would satisfy. Animals have none of our human sexual problems. They are not worried about orgasm, they don't "leer" at the opposite sex, or laugh at "dirty" jokes. They experience no guilt over these matters, require no sex therapists and have no problem repressing their physical urges. There are no animal prostitutes. But, by the same token, they cannot deeply love one another. Our problems arise when we try to force full satisfaction out of our animalistic tendencies when we are much more than animals. It is like trying to play a Beethoven symphony on a mouth organ. Persons who limit themselves in this way do not realize that genital sex is the signpost to something much richer and more satisfying.

Other couples go beyond genital sex but still do not go all the way because they stop at sexuality. This is the uniting of two personalities in which a high degree of meaningful love may be experienced and expressed. They have a sense of oneness with each other which overcomes to some degree the separateness of each and the loneliness of being half a person seeking for a mate. They can experience "coitus," which really means "to have relations with."

Let me illustrate. Well do I remember the night Anna and I first kissed. It was under the stars in a grassy area by many tall trees right beside a little waterfall, not far from a railway bridge. It took several days to gather up the necessary courage to take this tremendous and risky step. Would she refuse me? If so, I would certainly feel rejected. Would she laugh at me? I would feel like a fool. There was no way of telling. So without asking, I just up and did it. To my surprise and delight she accepted this, my first token of bursting affection. I felt like the man who wrote:

> Give me a kiss, add to that kiss a score;
> Then to that twenty, add a hundred more:
> A thousand to that hundred; so kiss on,
> To make that thousand up a million.
> Treble that million, and when that is done,
> Let's kiss afresh, as when we first begun.[23]

As I walked home that night I remember saying to myself, "She let me kiss her, she *really* let me kiss her." I was walking on air, my chest expanded, my head was dizzy with the promise of it all. But the words *"SHE let ME kiss HER,"* were a leap forward beyond the actual kiss. It was HER and ME. We had bridged a chasm of separateness. Our personalities had begun to merge. And when the long four years of courtship had finally passed, I discovered that it is this oneness of two personalities in love that gives meaning and fulfillment to genital union.

Still, there remains much pain even in the finest union of personalities and bodies, because human love even at its highest is still another pointer, a guidepost. Only as two people open their marriage to God and reach out to Him in yearning love does He in His Holy Spirit move into their hearts to complete the union, bringing heaven and earth together in a mysterious and marvelous cohesive whole. Then it is that a couple feel oneness with the entire universe. This is a little bit of heaven on earth and, in turn, is still another pointer to what possibilities await us in life after this life.

Genital and sexual union can now find their proper function: signposts for so much more. They can never be fulfilling in themselves. Even to try for that is a form of idolatry. When genital sex is idolized it turns to gravel in the mouth, something to spit out. Most prostitutes hate sex and despise their partners. This also is the lie that lurks in extra-marital relationships. Sex, a God-ordained activity much like the elements of holy communion, meant to be the ritual of love and complete union, is reduced to a matter of money, or mere physical release, or arrogant self-aggrandizement.

The person who said, "Sex is beautiful, why spoil it by getting married?" is the victim of "cinema mentality," the idea that romantic love ends with marriage. This is why so many movies and stories highlight the first stages of male-female relationship. This is the only exciting part in their view. Do they really think that when this is over the best part of the story is finished and all that remains is anticlimactic?

Only in the full commitment of spiritual union can the bursting flame of infatuation become the quiet, steady glow of increasing affection. A couple can now begin to move on into the adventure of growing tenderness and greater maturity. A woman wrote: "In the past five years we have lived abroad, progressed in our individual careers, given birth to two beautiful sons, have had fights, smiles, tears, great joys, moments of extreme closeness and times when we wondered what we ever saw in each other. In short, we have had a real marriage." Such are the ingredients that contribute to making marriage a constant, exciting and expanding discovery. There is always more ahead, more to understand, to experience, to give, to receive. More ways to mature.

In such a marriage the joy of quiet closeness is indescribable and there is no room for boredom. Is this what Jesus had in mind when he spoke of his joy being in us and our joy being full (John 15:11)? Did Paul point to this when he wrote of Him "who by the power at work within us is able to do far more abundantly than all that we ask or think" (Ephesians 3:20)?

Here, I believe, is an important key to being married and free, free to experience the depth of oneness without submerging individuality. Unity in diversity, separateness and togetherness, these become the alternate areas of growth. No need now to hold each other back because there is no jealousy or competition except in "showing honour to one another" (Romans 12:10).

Such a couple are now free to receive. There are three stages of expressing love verbally. The first says, "I love you," the second, "I love you, too," and the third, "Thank you for loving me." Only in the third do we continue to bask in the constant wonder and the persistent joy of being loved. This is sheer grace. It not only sets us free but keeps us free, free to bring forth the possibilities dormant within each other. It is freedom to affirm one another without flattery.

Some time ago I had an overnight stay in the hospital for tests. It took place over a Tuesday, garbage day at our place, and it usually falls to me to see that those big plastic bags are carried out to the street early in the morning. When I am absent from home, it could be overlooked, which only adds to the next week's pile. I have often been checked for reminding my family to put out the garbage.

But before leaving for the hospital I announced, ''Don't forget, Tuesday is garbage day!'' to which I got a rather disinterested response. I had an added reason for doing this. Because it was the first Tuesday in the month it was also paper day. To neglect putting those papers out for the recycling truck meant they accumulated for a whole month. So I felt justified, wise and fatherly!

From the hospital I phoned home. It was about 8 A.M. I was anxious to know if the garbage was out but hesitated to ask, realizing how they felt about this matter. At the same time Anna knew what was on my mind and was just stubborn enough at that particular moment not to give me the satisfaction of knowing.

We spoke of many minor things while all the time I felt she was just waiting for my ''plunge.'' I was hoping she would give in and provide the information without my having to bring it up. We talked on and on.

Then I remembered that I had seen one of her pictures hanging in the hospital reception area. So I blurted out. ''Did you know your painting is hanging downstairs right near the office? It's beautiful and brightens up the whole place.''

Immediately she responded, ''That's wonderful! Oh, and incidentally the garbage is out —and the papers too!''

What a touch of affirmation will do! Isn't it amazing?

By being enthusiastically in love with God, each other and life, two married people can maintain the spirit of happy laughter, playful exchange and spontaneous complementarity: the marks of youthfulness. This keeps marriage exciting. As one man said, ''We never have a dull lull!''

A couple who have discovered this ''more'' are free to bring out the best in each other. Part of the meaning of Christian marriage is to help one another to ''grow in grace and in the knowledge of our Lord and Savior Jesus Christ'' (2 Peter 3:18).

1978 was ''my year'' to have a heart attack. Some days in intensive care, then three weeks of rest under careful observation brought me to that great day when I prepared to go home. Needless to say, I was excited at the thought of being with my family once again and closer to Anna.

That morning my female physician came into my room for consultation, and amongst other things shocked me by saying, " . . . and after four weeks you can resume sex." I didn't know whether to thank her for the warning or to tell her to mind her own business. Did I detect a touch of humor in her voice? Anyway I can't remember how I responded but took it as just standard medical advice.

I thought those four weeks would be a deprivation, but to my happy surprise they turned out to be an unforeseen blessing. The doctor did not say we couldn't cuddle, hold, rejoice and pray! I thanked God for that. Setting the physical aside, we were able to share and communicate on a deeper level than we had known for some time. We enjoyed a kind of communion of spirits that was literally "out of this world." We leapt over the sexual aspect of our marriage into our individual and mutual relationship to God. In prayer we felt a oneness with the divine that in turn gave us new depths of appreciation and tenderness toward each other. Nothing else could have made that happen. We discovered a peaceful joy that even surpassed the remembered happiness of our wedding day. We were gripped by the insight of Scripture, "Do not refuse one another except perhaps by agreement for a season, that you may devote yourselves to prayer" (I Corinthians 7:5).

Yes, there is much more—and it is available to any couple in any marriage. One man who made this marvelous discovery said, "I only have one regret, I should have married her sooner." Well, it's a nice thought, but then we do have all of eternity.

THE SECRET

"A solid, long-lasting marriage has become so exquisitely rare that it's become interesting again. It's like the pearl in the oyster, or the white whale; it's like the snow leopard or some other species that's threatening to go extinct—it's become downright exotic."[24]

It's true! No institution has been as thoroughly probed, shaken, lambasted and put through the hoop of psychological and social pressure as has marriage. Still, many marriages not only survive, they thrive.

Do these have a secret? Probably they have one quality above all others—forgiveness. Marriage without forgiveness is like a car running without oil. The multiple moving parts simply grind away at each other creating heat and wear until the inevitable breakdown.

An incident from our own marriage which happened many years ago may show how a family crisis highlights the necessity of forgiveness. Our second son, Stanley, was just three. Playing with his older sister Jane, he came running toward her to share his apple. In his exuberance, and concentrating on what he had in his hand, he ran smack into the corner edge of an open door, falling away stunned and cut. Jane called for mother to come quickly. As Anna picked him up, he was crying hard, blood spurting from a deep, one-inch cut right in the centre of his forehead. Turning him over in her arms she carried him into the kitchen. Now I quote from Anna's diary (with her permission):

A handy teatowel mopped up the blood from his eyes and face. Now with both children crying loudly I phoned the doctor who said to turn up at his office in two hours, meanwhile to use a bandaid to hold the cut together.

The blood soon stopped coming as we laid him down on the bed. He

49

sobbed, "baby, baby." In a little while he tried to sit up and walk, but preferred resting.

The time at the doctor's office was an ordeal we'll long remember. I had to hold him while the "local" needles were put in. He kicked and screamed and struggled and must have been shocked at his mother forcing him to this and looking him straight in the eyes! I learned it is tough work to sew through skin, watching the stitches being put in with the curved needles and forceps.

It was all I could do to hold Stanley on the table, so frightened was he. For the last stitch the doctor wrapped a sheet around his legs. Then Stanley smiled and shook hands with the doctor, now that it was all over, as if to say, "well done Doc."

I felt weaker about it the next day as unused muscles rebelled. But as we prayed at bedtime and mealtime for Stan's safe restoration we had satisfaction and were assured too, the scar would not be bad.

When this happened Anna phoned me at the church office. I returned home but stayed with our older son John while she and Jane took Stan to the doctor's office. Two days later I chose again to separate myself from Anna when she had to take him back for a checkup, pleading an important meeting which, I told her, demanded my presence.

I again quote from the diary:

I almost persuaded him to come against his will and both of us were angry. I felt he could be absent from the meeting ten to fifteen minutes. I said crossly, "O.K., we'll go alone. It's time for us to be there now."

I hope he has forgiven and forgotten the incident as I've forgiven him now (9 P.M. the same evening) but I still feel disappointed. The traffic was heavy and we were lucky to get there safely. There is too much to be done to waste time on such thought. Time heals. So back to work. Too bad though, not to have been able to use this opportunity of a united family affair.

Such is the "stuff" of marriage and, much as we would like to correct our failures even after more than twenty-five years, it cannot be done. But, something much better can take place, and that is forgiveness. When we fail our mate, whether through unkindness, thoughtlessness or deliberate hurt, we place ourselves and the entire

50

relationship in their hands. But if they deny us forgiveness at this crucial time they cancel the one gift without which the marriage cannot continue in the same freedom and joy. A couple may pick up and go on dutifully pretending that everything is the same, but the relationship has been crippled. On the other hand, when forgiveness is freely offered and accepted, a relationship can breathe again and move forward to new heights of understanding both of self and of each other.

The alternative? How well married people know! Perhaps hours or even days of non-communication, unbelievable loneliness, a feeling of going nowhere, carrying a stone-heavy heart and that senseless competition to see who is going to break down first. It is at these times that the worst of our nature comes out. We become stubborn, proud, sullen. We start licking our wounds, our stomach is in knots, we give icy stares and suffer emotional isolation and sleepless nights. The conjugal bed then becomes a department of hell.

Yet so perverse and proud are we that we may deliberately choose that kind of torment rather than make a new beginning through the constructive act of forgiving one another. Such a marriage would be definitely sick, turning on revenge rather than reconciliation. Each partner then wants to humiliate the other—saying inwardly, "I'll bring him down a peg or two," or "I'll make her crawl." It then turns into a power-play in which each strives for the upper hand. Worse, it may descend into a regular knock'em down, drag'em out fight to the finish. Thus couples can emotionally drain each other. This can take place just so often until one or both come to the conclusion that it simply isn't worth the effort any more. By that time the end of the marriage is probably in sight.

A friend of mine who has had long experience in marriage counselling confronts almost everyone who seeks his help with one basic question. After they have unloaded their feelings, told all the bad points of their partner and tried to make clear their own innocence, he simply asks, "Do you want to be right or do you want to be well?"

He is offering two roads, one of self-justification and the other of healing and forgiveness. So long as they only want to be supported in their "rightness" he cannot assist them. If they want to be well, physically, emotionally and relationally, there is a way and it necessarily passes through forgiveness. One famous counsellor said, "Forgiveness is the greatest therapeutic idea in the world." Where does this all-important quality come from?

Paul says: "God's love [and forgiveness] has been poured into our hearts" (Romans 5:5). Once we have received this Divine Love we have such a confident sense of our own worth that we are no longer driven by the need to defend ourselves. Now we are freed to admit our guilt, confess our failure, acknowledge our weakness. We are free also to love sincerely, to identify with the feelings of our loved one, to imagine ourselves in their position and to offer forgiveness with no strings attached. We can only give what we have first received.

Marriage takes a gigantic leap toward freedom when both partners are liberated from always having to be right. No longer on the defensive, they don't feel that they diminish themselves by quickly saying, "I'm sorry," and meaning it.

A singer who always preferred to have his wife accompany him on the piano was heard to say, "She knows how to cover up for my mistakes." That is what marriage is, covering for one another and producing beautiful music together. Only free people can do that!

In the crisis mentioned above, Anna, consciously or unconsciously, put forth the essential steps in restoring our relationship. Let's look at these. "I hope by now he has forgiven." She had enough evidence of my ineptitude to clobber me and enough ammunition to accuse and blame me for weeks. But somehow she felt my failure with me, knowing that I was capable of better things, identifying with my inner feelings and making herself vulnerable to the extent of expressing her own need of my forgiving her. Did she feel guilt, too? Of what? I only know that whatever it was, it has long since been buried under the mound of emotional debris that every marriage accumulates.

She records that she spoke crossly, although I cannot remember that. Even if she did, it may have been just an outburst of pent-up feelings unrelated to the incident. I could think of a lot of things. Maybe she'd been feeling for weeks that I had not been spending enough time at home, that she had been carrying the burden alone, competing with my multiple church meetings. Life is often too complex to work out all the subconscious memories, thoughts, drives, defenses and resentments that clutter our path. The point is, rather than making pulp of me she began with herself and her own need of forgiveness, proof that she was inwardly a free person.

If nothing else would have convicted and melted me, this penitent attitude accomplished it, although she didn't do it for that reason. Ruling out any idea of competition, it was clear recognition that we are committed to each other in love, that we want to bear each other's burdens and share each other's joys.

". . . and forgotten," she continued. Paul said, "Love keeps no score of wrongs" (I Cor. 13:5 NEB). Why not? Because it doesn't want to and doesn't need to. The desire to hit back is gone along with the inner need to be forever proven right.

She writes on, ". . . as I've forgiven him,"—clearly indicating that she was in no way seeking to be a martyr but only wanting to pick up the pieces and get on with the business of living. Sometimes there is nothing else we can do. As she wrote later: "There is too much to be done to waste time. Time heals. So back to work."

Incidents such as I've described do take place in marriage but they should not be permitted to throw things out of perspective long enough to form fixed attitudes. It is important to get back on the rails as soon as possible. Anna's decision to forgive was her investment in that goal. It started the healing process immediately.

She ends the account with this very human touch, "But I still feel disappointed . . . Too bad not to have been able to use this opportunity of a united family affair." Marriage can be strengthened by crises, depending entirely on how they are met and used. Because she both asked for and offered forgiveness, and because later on I was able, by God's grace, to do the same, we were more in love than before our little son ever hit that door. Both of us were a bit more mature, more sensitive to one another, and more certain of our relationship.

A woman said, "I remember only the good times and try to forget the bad." Great, but forgiveness goes beyond that and turns the bad times into good and everything ends up on the side of a stronger marriage and new-found joy.

This joy is immeasurable because we now have something tremendous to celebrate, triumph over our failures. This is life's *real party* in which we celebrate release from pent-up resentment, from the bondage of hurt pride and the weight of a mound of accumulated misunderstandings. It is made possible because we are convinced that God has released us individually through His love. All of this marks the beginning of something new and more exciting than was ever thought possible before, that two people now no longer vying for ascendency can laugh and love and live out their human frailties together.

There is a good word in the book of Ecclesiastes: "Two are better than one . . . for if they fall one will lift up his fellow . . . but woe to him who is alone when he falls and has not another to lift him up" (Eccles. 4:9-10). In a good marriage, one that is free, we are constantly in the business of lifting each other up.

Who said it would be easy? One would think that the more we love the easier it would be to forgive. The opposite is the truth. Anna loves me but that night she also felt her deep maternal love for Stanley, identified with him in his injury, being sensitive to every puncture of the needle in his head-wound. If it could be measured, she probably suffered more than the child. All of that cannot be brushed off easily. She couldn't turn to me after the ordeal was over and say, "Oh well, let's just forget it," then make up and pretend it didn't happen. She was hurt in Stanley's hurting, and hurt further by my neglect. Double love meant double pain.

All this brings lovers close to the meaning of the cross of Christ, the most important event that ever took place on planet Earth. If God is the Divine Lover He is also the Divine Sufferer and, by the same token, the Divine Forgiver. This is the price of genuine love and it is at the very centre of the meaning of our existence. If marriage is "the great school," then our essential lesson is the meaning of real love, as we discover that what we must go through on a human level, God goes through infinitely on the divine level.

But it doesn't end there. It goes on to resurrection, new life, joy. Marriage in this process of dying and being raised to new life can know a peaceful happiness and freedom unattainable in any other way. We can now know we are loved unconditionally and there arises within such an overwhelming sense of gratitude, that we, in turn, are motivated to respond in the same way. So Paul says, "Be kind to one another, tenderhearted, forgiving one another, *as God in Christ has forgiven you*" [Emphasis mine] (Ephesians 4:32).

Jesus said that He had come to "set at liberty those who are bruised" (Luke 4:15). Marriage is a series of bruises, some deliberate, most unintentional. Forgiving and being forgiven is the key to a dimension of freedom and gladness beyond words to describe.

The question is, how long can we keep this up, especially if response is slow to come? Well, Peter raised that question. "How often shall I forgive?'' he asked Jesus. Then he put forth his own answer which he probabely thought was quite generous, ''Seven times?'' Jesus replied, ''No, but seventy times seven'' (Matthew 18:21-22). Forgiveness, if it is sincere, must be unlimited. In marriage it is the daily diet and there can be no substitute and no giving up.

There would seem to be at least six stages.

1. ''I won't forgive — you can stew in your own juice.'' What one doesn't realize here is that he or she is already stewing in a juice of their own making. It's like cutting off your head to get rid of a headache.

2. ''I should forgive but I don't want to.'' Usually this attitude is sheer pride. Reality therapy would pose the question, ''Then what do you really want? The hell of unforgiveness? Consider that!''

3. ''I really want to but it is too difficult.'' This is understandable because only the loved person can love and only the forgiven can forgive.

4. ''I'll forgive but on the condition you beg for it.'' This is a case of seeking status. It smacks of, ''Your failure proves me right. My strength demands your weakness. When you grovel in the dust at my feet, I'll then consider being the big-hearted forgiver so you will be at my mercy. I may have a few faults, but it is clear you have more and bigger ones.''

5. ''I'll forgive if you will do the same.'' This is the BARGAIN approach. If each partner took the same stance the marriage would be deadlocked.

6. ''I'll offer it to you as a free gift because I am forgiven by God.'' No response is demanded. ''Whether or not my forgiveness is accepted and whether or not you respond in the same way is not the issue. Here is my gift to you because I truly love you. I want you to be free so that we can both discover higher joys as our marriage becomes more and more the exciting adventure it already is.''

Every marriage partner must make a choice and it's a case of ''make your bed and lie in it.'' The consequences of not forgiving can be horrendous. But the great discovery is that forgiveness, freely offered on a day-by-day basis is the secret of being truly free.

BEYOND THE FLESH

An advertisement for a current movie says: "THERE'S MORE TO LOVE THAN MAKING LOVE." I take this as an open admission that, in spite of the modern trend toward libertinism in matters of sexual conduct and in the face of all the supposedly new modes of experimentation in the sexual field, hordes of people feel they are missing something. What is it?

Saturated with the Playboy philosophy, inundated with tales of glamorous people who appear happy on the glossy pages of slick magazines even as they continue in their game of musical beds, and surrounded as we are by reports of marriage breakup in the lives of those from whom we should least expect it, all would seem to confirm the fact that something must be lacking in our understanding of what sex is all about.

Striking a match starts a fire, but it takes more than the match to keep it going. Physical attraction, hunger for attention, security or status, et cetera, may bring a couple together, but there has to be a constant supply of fuel to maintain and strengthen their relationship, or else, like the fire, it will die.

I propose that what is needed is "soul." Forget all those shadowy images we've had about our soul, as if it were some blob inside us somewhere, a part of us set aside for "religion" which will somehow be released when we die. A surgeon once cut up a body and reported that he found no trace of a soul. What did he expect? Or what did the Russian cosmonaut expect to see when he went up into space and reported that he couldn't find God?

"Soul" is the distilled essence of something. It is truth, reality, substance, intrinsic nature. Our soul is our true identity, the real person inside. Jesus said, "What good is it if you gain the world but lose your soul [your identity, your true self]?" (Mark 8:36).

The various parts of life, of which sex is one, must in some way be integrated with this basic essence of our selves. We are not bodies that have souls but essentially we are souls that, for our use in this world, have bodies. To isolate sex or to exalt it above its relative position in the whole self is to invite self-defeat. The famous psychiatrist Carl Jung wrote: "Sexuality released as sexuality is brutish. But as an expression of love sexuality is hallowed."[25]

We can demonstrate this from experience. When there is some unsettled question between husband and wife, or when one party is waiting for an apology, or when one is feeling rejected, satisfying the senses is virtually impossible. This is not the case with animals. The instinct, the release, the physical act, is all that is necessary. Feelings, relationships, hurt memories and a sense of self-worth never enter into their sex life. However, before the sex act can be a fulfilling experience for humans there must be "soul." It must all somehow contribute to the overall sense of well-being, harmony, self-esteem, and oneness, strengthening the bond that links two lives together. This is why affection expressed through touching, holding, waiting, kissing and caressing is so important. This is not just foreplay. It must be real in itself so that if and when the sex act takes place it becomes the celebration of what has already been solidly established—the oneness of two souls.

People talk about "making love," as if the sex act could do just that. Well, if a couple are not already in love, sex by itself will not create it. Sex is then devastating to their sense of self-worth. Passion alone may carry each of them for the moment, but the aftermath is disillusionment, loneliness and rejection. Yet many, not realizing that they are primarily souls that have bodies, continue to search for self-fulfillment in the physical act itself, an impossible achievement.

The Bible helps us here, for it is very explicit concerning the origin, purpose, meaning, beauty and possibilities of sex as well as its dangers, perversions, temptations. The Bible glories in this God-given aspect of our lives and shows how it can be heightened, dignified and made sacred by being set in the framework of permanent relationship, marked by faithfulness that reflects the faithfulness of God himself. Far from denigrating it, the Bible says, in effect, sex is too wonderful a thing to be taken casually. Held in reverence before God it will contribute immeasurably to human fulfillment. Practised independently of "soul" it becomes ugly, hateful and destructive. This is the experience of the race and it is true not just because it is in the Bible. It is in the Bible because it is true.

The Bible states unequivocally that we are made *by* God (we didn't just "happen" but are part of a divine plan), we are made *like* God (we have something of divinity within us), and we are made *for* God (our real life is only attained when we reflect His nature and purpose). Life, then, has a spiritual base, a fact perhaps that is more evident in a good marriage than anywhere else because here is where life is most intimately personal.

Someone has noted the fact that at the lowest level of existence there is least emphasis on sex as passion and relationship, and at this level the highest fertility occurs. The salmon will lay four million eggs but never meets her mate. Animals meet in procreation but not permanently. Their offspring are greatly reduced in number. But when you come to humans, sex is not just physical union but is deeply emotional and spiritual, infinitely more than mere instinct. So it would look as if for the lower creatures the sex urge finds its impetus from below, pushing for the propagation of the species. But in people, made in the image of God, there is an urge from above for spiritual union.

We are intuitively spiritual. Some years ago there was a popular movie about a beautiful girl who was in love with three fellows at the same time. Which one to marry? One was a rich and handsome man who brought out the woman in her. She was proud of him and it was obvious that if she were to choose him she would have no lack of every material thing she could desire. The next wasn't rich but was filled with enthusiasm. She liked that and dreamed that life with him would be exciting and fun. The third didn't seem to have very much that was obvious. He wasn't rich, had few talents and was anything but "tall, dark and handsome"—just your average, ordinary "good guy." But when he kissed her she heard strange and beautiful music. Smart girl that she was, she married this man. She had listened to her soul.

Today we are being swamped by theories of sex that disdain anything spiritual. The media is very successful in saturating society with a view of sex as being only physical and with the notion that satisfaction is to be found merely through the union of sex organs. Much of this would seem to come from secular psychologists, many of whom base their opinions on experiments with pigeons or mice. One even told how we should handle human sexuality based on his observations of potato bugs. He forgot to take into account one small fact—we are not bugs.

The result is more frustration today then ever before. Sex education doesn't help here, nor does the new spirit of openness and frankness about discussing the subject with anyone, even grade-school children. And amongst the most sexually mauled-over there is a kind of cynicism about the whole subject that is sad indeed.

Marriage? Well, the best they can say for it is that it may be o.k. for birds. Judy Collins told a TV audience that the only benefits she could see in marriage were the tax breaks. "I grew up with the old-fashioned hangover about marriage as something you're supposed to do," she said, "and so the fantasy floated in my mind for years. But now it's gone. It simply died its own death. I'm not interested in it."[26] One writer said, "Marriage may be compared to a cage. The birds outside despair to get in and those within despair to get out."

Therefore, sex, to be fulfilling, must be understood within the context of spirit or soul, or else it will sabotage itself. The great philosopher Plato told of the crew of a certain ship who decided that their pilot must be mad because he took observations from the stars. They argued that a ship sails on seas and is influenced by the winds and tides and currents, and that stargazing is a foolish, impractical procedure. They seized him and shut him up in the ship's hold; then they sailed right onto the rocks. So with sex: we must take our readings from that which is beyond what can be seen and sensed through the physical alone.

Some would write off the idea of "soul" as being just a socially propagated idea without substance in fact. But experience and honest thinking drives us to the position that the spiritual is reality, written into our very nature, an essential and unavoidable aspect of our true humanity.

For instance, here is a young couple who refused to believe all this talk about conscience and standards. Right and wrong to them were simply reduced to how they personally felt about things. "Anything is right," they said, "providing you are not hurting anybody else." So they went their way and did their thing. Their objective was plainly sexual and they went at it with youthful zest.

But after a while the novelty wore off. Each sex experience was reduced to "just another time," and he began to crave variety while she hungered for deeper affection. He resented some of her questions about his real motives and she was jealous of his possible alliance with others. Finally they agreed to part, but not without a good deal of inner hurt. Later she said to her pastor, "I told him all my secrets and he just walked away! I don't think I could trust anybody like that again." She was thoroughly disillusioned.

When a man and a woman become "soul mates," they have a

60

dimension in their relationship that enhances everything else. One woman put it: "We find over and over again that there is a 'given' quality about marriage, as there is of any of the intangible satisfactions of life. It is a gift of God we don't deserve. It gets more wonderful all the time, as we grow in understanding and appreciation of each other. As it was when we started this adventure under God, so it is repeatedly now; when we surrender our self-centred demands, God gives us back something more wonderful than we had ever thought of. There is something about it we do not make ourselves, and could not make or demand or get by any means of our own; we feel it is given from above, as are all good gifts; it is right and free and happy; it is a share in God's redeeming grace."

One obvious result of this is that sexual relations improve. Not long ago two married people who are "experts" in the marriage field, counsellors and authors of many books on marriage were interviewed on TV. They said, "Christians should be the sexiest and most turned on people in the world."[28] This might surprise many people, but it's true, a fact to which multitudes could witness with resounding enthusiasm.

Redbook magazine printed an analysis of 18,349 responses, mostly from middle-class mothers, to a professionally prepared questionnaire on sexual attitudes and practises. It showed that "strongly religious" women received more sexual satisfaction, had more orgasms and better communication with their husbands than "fairly religious" women. At the bottom of the happiness scale were the non-religious. They were the least satisfied with the quality and frequency of intercourse and the least likely to take an active role in lovemaking.[29]

Religious women, it was discovered, have the greatest capacity to let themselves go. Because of a positive world-view, they have better feelings about themselves and about their sexuality. All of life fits together better for them. They have an integrating view, a scheme of things, their sexual behavior not being divorced from all other human meanings. This is described as sexual liberation and it is a good gift of God. Their abiding sense of self-worth makes for sex at its best, reflecting commitment, shared values, mutual respect and meaningful intimacy.

Some time ago I spent three weeks speaking in churches in the Caribbean. Normally I am not away from home for that long a stretch, but I have found that when I am, the heart grows fonder. I long for fellowship with my wife and the family as the days slowly pass. On this occasion Anna met me at the airport and we had the usual affectionate greeting. Then as we proceeded homeward we talked about all the family events that had taken place since I had left—items of news, messages and the like. Arriving home at last, I was tired and wanted to proceed hurriedly to bed. But no, Anna had planned something else.

She made me sit down in the living room and in a few moments came from the kitchen with a tray on which were two crystal glasses and a flask of homemade grape juice along with a bit of bread she had baked that day. I said, "But I'm not hungry. I ate on the plane."

"This is not a meal," she replied. "It's communion."

The very last thing I would have thought about was the sacrament, and I confess that it took me so much by surprise that I needed a few minutes to warm up to the idea. Then I saw her point. We are soul-mates.

It was very brief and informal with no prescribed ritual. But spontaneously from our hearts we began to confess weaknesses, thoughtless acts, indifference and remembered times of selfishness. We felt our Lord's presence. We sensed His arms around us both. We quoted a few verses of Scripture. We then shared the bread and the juice with a quiet reverence that seemed to gather up all the highest and loveliest thoughts we had ever had toward each other and made them live in the present moment. We prayed. We wept a little, for joy. We had an overwhelming sense of thankfulness for life, for each other, for family and home and work and friends. We were grateful for safety in travel and for God's protecting love. It was one of my life's unforgettable moments and will linger in my mind as a beautiful and precious memory. We enthusiastically recommend to others: eat and drink—in remembrance of our Lord.

After communion and still in the mood of prayer, we tumbled into bed. It was not a matter of "making love" but of celebrating love that was deep and all-embracing and eternal. Both of us were affirmed, re-created, cherished. Afterwards we felt united with the Eternal as we revelled in God's presence in receptive silence. We were renewed, "lost in wonder, love and praise."

All of this is a far, far cry from the world's emphasis on "performance." There was no question of release or passion or possible failure. Physical considerations were overcome in the full experience of love which words fail to describe.

On one occasion we washed each other's feet as a symbol of our "being subject to one another out of reverence for Christ" (Ephesians 5:21).

This is what I believe God intends the marriage relationship to be and I, for one, desire it to be that way always. It is not necessary to have communion as we did. Sometimes in the midst of the physical act itself, it is wonderful to stop, rest, think and pray, opening both persons to God and involving Him in the union. He then gives of Himself, blessing and heightening the moment to a level of indescribable joy.

The Bible says, "Glorify God in your bodies" (I Corinthians 6:20). When we glorify God through our sexual union, He glorifies us toward our highest fulfillment.

I was in a group in which a woman expressed her jealousy of the time her husband was giving to the church. But after deep thought and conversation with a friend she gained a new perspective on this and prayed, "Thank you God that Tom loves You more than he does me, and because he loves You so much I know he loves me the more."
Before his marriage a man wrote this prayer in his diary:

That I may come near to her, draw me nearer to Thee than to her; that I may know her, make me to know Thee more than her; that I may love her with the perfect love of a perfectly whole heart, cause me to love Thee more than her and most of all. That nothing may be between me and her, be Thou between us every moment. That we may be constantly together, draw us into separate loneliness with Thyself. And when we meet breast to breast, O God, let it be upon Thine own.[30]

This kind of intimacy is infinitely closer than sex, becoming the celebration of love in all its dimensions, not merely the means of "making love." For love cannot be "made." It must be given and received. It must be nurtured in trust. It is the ground of intimacy, and intimacy enhances love, that mutually wonderful experience of being real close.
It goes beyond the flesh.

THE OLD CANOE

At our cottage we have an old canoe. I mean it's very old, perhaps seventy-five years. It would be a genuine antique if I hadn't had it fiberglassed. Five generations of Hunters have paddled that same canoe.

Nobody could tell how often it had been rubbed, sanded, varnished and painted. One summer day I bestirred myself to do it again as it had been long neglected.

I hauled it up on wooden horses and proceeded to scrape and sand. The inside wood was almost black with the accumulation of so many coats slapped on by previous unskilled craftsmen like myself.

Figuring I had worked long enough in the sun and had smoothed the wood sufficiently, I diligently opened a fresh can of varnish and began spreading on the gleaming new surface, thoroughly enjoying myself and taking no little pride in my loving care for this family heirloom.

Just then Anna came down the pathway. It took only a few moments for her to survey the situation and volunteer her opinion. "Why didn't you take it right down to the wood?" she asked.

"Because I haven't time," I responded rather indifferently, "and besides, nobody else has ever done that before so why do it now?"

She insisted. Through her many words I could sense what was probably going on in her mind and it made me cringe. I imagined her thinking, "What kind of a workman are you, anyway? That's the trouble. You always do things in halves. You don't do a job right. This will all have to be done over, including what you've just put on," (which I thought looked so nice).

She then took hold of some sandpaper and proceeded to show me how, with a little elbow grease, we could get right down to the wood and do a really nice job, making it like new.

But I was hurt, angered, and refused to listen. Whose project was

65

this, anyway? Why did she have to come on the scene and interfere just when I was doing so nicely, and enjoying myself? Does she not have plenty of projects of her own?

I continued to strengthen my defense, so I said to myself, "The canoe is too old and too far gone now to try to restore it to the original. My holidays are too short to let this job take more than a minimum of hours. Anyway, I'm not a professional or specialist at restoring old canoes. I want to get this over with and get on to the next job demanding to be done around our place."

So I kept on. Anna backed off and returned to the cottage, probably steaming inside of herself and saying, "Men! They're all the same! They just won't change."

However, that wasn't the end of the incident because, as in so many cases, it raised the whole matter of our relationship, of the nature of marriage and of what love might mean in a situation like this. After I cooled down a little I could see that she was on track, as she usually is, but I wasn't prepared to let her show me up. She was basically right in suggesting that no job is worth doing that isn't worth doing well, and also in her assessment of my abilities as a bungling craftsman. That, I would not deny. Too many half-done things around our place bear witness.

But we were both right. Some jobs are not worth doing too well, demanding too much effort and time. Sometimes it's either half-a-job or nothing. In this situation, taking all things into consideration—I was convinced that I was doing the reasonable thing.

Then why did the undeclared war between us continue through that day until sometime into the night? I tossed and turned, thinking, "It's all so silly. Why let incidents like this spoil our relationship?" So I slowly slipped my arm around her. She responded immediately, thus indicating that similar thoughts had come to her as well.

Out of this mess I learned something about marriage, and that is the importance of *patience*. Patience is like yeast in dough. It is not a reacting quality, but rather a positive virtue which promotes change.

I have an idea that many marriages are hung up at just this point. Each is trying to change the other while denying the gift of patience, the very quality necessary for change to take place. A man said, "My wife and I have given up shopping together. When I go to the store I know what I want, find it, pay for it and bring it home. But my wife has no idea what she wants, stops and lingers over a counter, and when I ask if there is anything specific she wants she simply says, 'No, just looking.' This situation led to so many irritations that we simply shop on our own." Perhaps this is a first step in patience, that is, releasing each other from irritating situations, respectfully acknowledging our differences without criticism, sarcasm or ridicule.

Marriage has been called "the impossible commitment." It is a marvel that so many get on as well as they do, given the combination of two distinctly different personalities, brought up in separate homes, having unlike tastes and divergent interests. Each brings his or her own bagful of personal habits, pet ideas and ways of doing things which are bound to cause conflict.

Take the case of Joe and Margaret. They got married to spite their parents' objections. Within the first week they discovered some appalling differences in tastes. Joe liked to sleep with the bedroom window open while Margaret thought that an open window was an invitation to pneumonia. He was a meat-and-potatoes man while she liked fancy foods. He tended to be a morning person, full of energy when the day broke but running down gradually through the day and ready for bed early at night. She was a night person, never fully awake until the sun went down. He liked peace, quiet and one symphony concert a week. She liked dancing, the movies and lots of company.

My guess is that when two people such as these manage through it all to rise above everything that would otherwise militate against their union and find positive joy in marriage, it is because each has learned to give the gift of patience to the other.

I used to think of patience as just dutifully putting in time. Until something happened or someone arrived, patience was the fill-in, often given grudgingly. Now I see it as a most valuable attitude by which both persons can be freed to change and grow. It is not just putting up with the faults, weaknesses, pecularities and irritating habits of another person. These are seen as temporary stopping-places on the way to freedom and maturity.

The Bible says, "Love is patient" (I Corinthians 13:4). It often grows out of irritation and is more precious in a marriage than the finest diamond. It helps hold two imperfect persons together as they realistically face up to each other's idiosyncrasies and immaturities. With patience they are willing to accept these as being part of the "deal" that marriage is.

If we are lacking in patience we place our mate under pressure to change. A woman said, "When I got married I didn't realize that deep down inside me was an attitude I would never have expressed to my husband. I carried it unconsciously though it expressed itself in many subtle, unrecognized and damaging ways. My dominant idea was, 'You're going to change.' I thought of my husband as a lump of clay that I had to mold and shape and re-design. No wonder he rebelled and accused me of nagging. With my conscious mind I accepted him and said so, but with my unconscious I was determined to make him shape up.''

To give patience is to recognize the fact that we are all persons "in the making." Marriage is never a state of having arrived, but is forever on the way. Many folk miss this because while they've heard it said, "The two shall become one," they think of this as a state rather than a promise. That phrase from Matthew 19:5 accurately describes what has happened, what is happening and what will happen through the years. The marriage ceremony makes them one in commitment, intention and goal, and creates the home. But through the years, providing they choose to grow, they enter more and more into unity of spirit and maturity in love.

Couples, not realizing this, are surprised and hurt when sharp differences arise. Expecting timeless bliss, they now wonder if they were meant for each other at all. Perhaps they thought of marriage as a contract binding them into a fixed and permanent mold. But marriage is never that. It is a covenant in which two people pledge to move forward together through all the changing future.

Like the Chinese symbol of yin and yang, the comma and the inverted comma together filling the entire circle, marriage is an ever-evolving process as each part learns to complement and balance the other. Patience with each other is the one necessary quality to facilitate this process. Without patience, not only is inner harmony disrupted, but the entire circle, the marriage itself, is threatened.

It is false to say that "love is blind." Perhaps puppy love is, but mature love sees in the marriage partner one who fulfills the personality needs and deficiencies in himself. Patience enhances the uniqueness of each individual; this contributes to the equilibrium of the whole, creating poise and counterpoise.

Much marriage breakup is caused by fear of losing personal identity and separateness. To be sure we want to be one, but not at the expense of our individuality. But the yin-yang idea, interfused with genuine patience, calls forth our respect for differences that would otherwise divide. A couple can now glory in each other's uniqueness and move on to discover individually more and more of their own distinctive personality.

Patience is not waiting for the other person to change into our image of what they should be and do. It is a gift to the other, setting them free to be themselves right now and to move toward their own highest image of themselves, a positive and exciting adventure into the possibilities of becoming.

Something else emerges from this and it is the deeper awareness that in God's plan, the two are definitely meant for each other and that this goes far beyond surface niceties. Out of the agonies and ecstasies of marriage each is discovering through the gift of patience that something solid and satisfying is being established at the core of their relationship. This increasingly becomes a source of security and peace.

Perhaps the most difficult persons to live with are the perfectionists who cannot or will not give the precious gift of patience. They think of themselves as faultless and that others should conform to their example. A woman said to her mate, "Darling, if you weren't such a perfectionist, you'd be a perfect husband." Such an attitude leads to rigidity and resistance, conflict and constant irritation which play havoc not only with the marriage relationship, but eventually with the mental and physical health of both parties.

Martin Luther said that marriage is a school for character. "All my life is patience," he said, thinking of his home and his wife, Katie. Yet he recognized that it was good for him, for it taught him this invaluable quality of character.[31]

It has been said that love is not the sudden pang of passion as with Romeo and Juliet, but in the last analysis it comes much closer to being the fond, sardonic, familiar and somewhat indulgent smile which a rapidly balding middle-aged man casts upon a wife who, sleepy-eyed and still in curlers, has just cooked the soft-boiled eggs a little too long for the 300th time over the years. It is the unselfish regard of a woman for a man whom she loved even more, if possible, the time he was out of work and the family lived on baked beans. True love can best be recognized by the fact that it thrives under circumstances which would blast anything else into small pieces. This kind of marriage takes patience, each partner being willing to absorb the deficiencies of the other, and doing it with a light heart.

What is the difference between loving and liking? One woman answered, "Love is the same as like except you feel sexier ... and more romantic ... and also more annoyed when he talks with his mouth full. It's only when you really love that you can resent it more when he interrupts you. And when you ask him to pick you up at the airport and he tells you that he can't do it because he's busy, it's only when you love him that you hate him." A mix-up of words? No! Just a statement showing the irony of marriage and the security of love that can risk expressing honest feelings because there is the background of patience that, in turn, calls forth the patience of the other, all ending in good humour.

Patience is a gift of God, one of the fruits of His Holy Spirit within (Galatians 5:22), and it must be received daily. Over an airlines counter I saw this sign: WE HAVE TO EARN OUR WINGS EVERY DAY. It startled me. As I thought about it the message grew in my mind. There are many things that have to be earned, given or received every day. Nothing stays won. The qualities that make a good marriage in which people find freedom to be and let be are not given once and for all. Patience must become a daily offering in the name of love to the one we love and who loves us.

We don't have to manufacture occasions in order to make this gift. Just living together will provide enough situations to call forth our patience, which in turn will liberate both partners toward their own beginning.

HOW TO DRIVE EACH OTHER SANE!

Most Christian ministers find themselves involved in a good deal of marriage counselling. They know the stories, the complaints and the heart-breaks. A few that stand out in my memory went like this:

—I've reached the end of my rope and if I don't leave him soon I'll go stark raving mad.

—I didn't want to see the break-up of our marriage but many months ago I could see that it had really gone around the bend.

—She had me climbing the walls.

—The situation was hopeless, we'd long since reached a dead end.

—One morning I looked at myself in the mirror and was horrified to see how I'd aged because of our constant quarreling. We were totally incompatible. So I told myself that if I didn't get out now I'd go completely bananas.

In almost every case of exasperation in the face of seemingly impossible marital situations, I longed to communicate one very simple and fundamental fact, the need for a spiritual base. Most of these couples had no thought of God, little conscience, no "central frame of reverence." and few goals beyond individual happiness. They wanted advise, not accountability, a pat answer, not rearranging their whole value system. Couples who have been willing to face up to these basic needs have discovered how to contribute to each other's sanity enabling them to progress toward greater wholeness, peace of mind and joy in their marriage relationship.

A prime example is the man whose name was Legion (Luke 8:26-39). It was said that he was "possessed by demons," whatever that means. He was insane, no longer one person but an army of fighting persons inside. You might say he was a civil war, anti-social, violent. But after his encounter with Jesus, "He was sitting at the feet of Jesus, clothed and in his right mind." Surrendered to Jesus, people move from being abnormal to being sane. He finds us distraught, fighting ourselves and others, sick in mind and the victim of our own self-centredness. He leaves us poised, clear headed, redirected. He is Lord of wholeness, be it for an individual or a marriage.

He Himself is not only sanctity but divine sanity. Everywhere down the line of human experience He is turning out to be right. His entering into humanity has set a standard of character and conduct for all mankind for all time. Coleridge said, "Beyond what we see in Christ the human race will never progress."[32] The psychologist Professor Ernest Ligon said, "Christ is the soundest psychologist ever to guide human behavior."[33] Dr. Sadler, the psychiatrist, said, "Some day our ... scientific development ... may catch up with the teaching of the Man of Galilee."[34] And H.G. Wells said, "I must confess as an historian, this penniless preacher from Galilee is irresistably the centre of history."[35]

Every creature finds freedom in its natural element. A fish is free in water, a bird in the air and a worm in the soil. It can then obey the laws of its inner being. Now the Christian is convinced that we are made by God and for God and can only be free in God (Acts 17:24-28). When we refuse and rebel we are out of our element. Evil is the word *live* spelled backwards, so evil is anti-life, an attempt to live against the grain of the universe. Jesus Christ through His offer of divine forgiveness enables us to return home, where we belong, to come again into tune with God our Father and to breathe the free air of His Kingdom.

When these facts are applied to marriage it makes all the difference. Marriage then finds its "soul" and centre, its point of reference.

One of the best known psychotherapists in the world today is Dr. Rollo May. The opening sentence of one of his many books is just this: "People suffer personality breakdown because they do not have meaning in their lives."[36] The same could be said of a marriage. If a marriage is to live it must have meaning, purpose, goals and direction.

Moreover, when a couple surrender their marriage to Jesus as Lord, it will reflect His spirit, His compassionate love and His gracious forgiveness. It will be marked by tenderness, kindliness and caring, the kind of atmosphere in which persons find themselves uplifted and affirmed.

In this type of marriage a couple is involved in the one "triangle" that strengthens their relationship. And when they do surrender themselves to God in Christ, they discover that God also commits Himself to them, pours in His power, guidance and love, which keeps the marriage continually refreshed.

The experience of Bob and June makes it clear. Bob complained that June had never really left her parents. They controlled her to the point that he felt like an outsider. Every Sunday they had to have dinner with "Mom and Pop." Once he tried to kiss her in front of her parents but she turned away because she "wasn't to show affection in front of them."

June found sex distasteful. She was cold so that eventually their times of togetherness drew farther and farther apart until they were only a few times in a year. Bob put up with this as long as he could and finally decided to move to a new area and find another job. June followed a few months later and they tried to start over again but it was soon evident they were growing even further apart. Then, in his new work, Bob found himself strongly drawn to one particular woman who seemed to be fun-loving and free-spirited—everything June was not. So when June took the children home for a summer vacation, Bob moved in with his new companion, who had just recently left her husband.

"It bothered me at first," says Bob. "I knew adultery was wrong but as I read the Bible I kept telling myself that God forgave David his sin against Bathsheba and surely he would forgive me too. More than that, I reasoned that God wanted me to be happy, a Christian was supposed to be happy and since I hadn't been happy with my wife I was justified in finding someone else who would make me happy."

When June returned Bob asked her for a divorce, convinced that it was all over. Their marriage was finished. One night Bob and his new woman were sitting in a restaurant, when all of a sudden Bob lost his appetite. He knew that something was terribly wrong. He had been reading his Bible and trying to put the pieces of his life together but nothing would fit. Now, when he went to bed he could not sleep. The next day as they walked on the beach he bared his conscience and expressed his guilt about their whole affair.

"Where do you get these ideas?" she asked.

"From the Bible," Bob replied.

"That's rotten stuff," she shot back. "Don't you ever read that book again."

Bob says that right there she changed before his eyes. She was no longer the free, happy, delightful person he thought he had seen in her. She turned from him in anger, marched back to their cottage, gathered her things and drove off.

Bob returned home, phoned his wife at work and said, "Come back, I'm a broken man." He hung up, fell on the floor in the family room and cried for several hours. When June came in she just sat and watched. When the tears were finally spent he looked up and began to see her in a whole new light. She was beautiful!

"Whatever happened," Bob says, "God had done. He had taken the scales off my eyes; he had turned me right side up overnight. I never have had any desire to be with the other woman since then. I have fallen in love with June all over again."

It took a long time for June to rebuild her trust and even longer to be comfortable with sexual intimacy. But it was instant change for Bob and never did he doubt that they could build together a very satisfying relationship.

Now June tells her side: "Those months that Bob was away were terribly difficult. At times I thought I would die, the pain of rejection was so great. I thought we were doing what Christians are supposed to do. We read the Bible, we prayed together, we went to Church. But I had no concept of what an intimate relationship should be with my husband. I was reproducing what I had experienced from my parents and that was far from intimate.

"I was eaten up with resentment and suspicion. I felt the problem was entirely his. It took me ten months to see that I was the problem and I was filled with remorse for what I had done to Bob. He was so starved for love that he had to go against his Christian upbringing and even his own nature to gain a feeling of personal worth.

"Then the 'miracle day' came when Bob came back. I believed all along that God would do something but I didn't know how or when. When at last we were able to talk, with no assurance that there would be any change on my part at all, Bob committed himself to making our relationship work. I, who had thought myself the strong·

one, was definitely the one who needed healing.

"We did a lot of thinking and reading the Bible, this time not for doctrines but for healing of relationships. We read many books on relating as Christians which strengthened us. I read that sex was good and that God meant me to enjoy it. Then I began to think of ways to be more creative in loving my husband. I had lost my self-esteem and felt so worthless during the time Bob was away. Only now do I feel together emotionally. There is a wholeness about me I had never known before.

"What we've been through has been invaluable. I discovered that people who are locked into rigid patterns of living as we were have to take drastic measures in order to get out. We've learned how to use the tools of transactional analysis, parent effectiveness training and communication skills. These tools have been combined with prayer and our Christian commitment to marriage. So much has happened to us that now we are sharing with other couples and families, and this has now become our mission. We share what God has done for us at every opportunity. We're having the time of our lives."[37]

Isn't it amazing what God can do in a marriage when a couple hand over to Him all the pieces? Note that all the way through their great difficulties and time of separation, they still had God at the centre of their thinking. In Bob it resulted first in his guilty conscience. That was the negative side. On the positive side he says that God took the scales from his eyes and turned him right side up. This gave him a perspective on what was happening and what should happen. It also led to his new determination and commitment to make his marriage work. But perhaps the key to his changing is in his own words to his wife: "I'm a broken man."

Only God can break through our pride and deal with our guilt and troubled consciences when we are willing to be broken.

God was also at work in June who had to be broken as well, in order that after ten painful months she could come to the place of saying, "I'm the problem. I'm the one that needs healing." Both Bob and June had experienced the miracle of rebirth. Each of them became an illustration of Jesus' words, "Whoever would save his life will lose it, and whoever loses his life for my sake will find it" (Luke 16:25). This has been called the deepest law of life. It reveals the fact that until we are willing to die to ourselves we cannot live with others, or ourselves.

75

With God at the centre both Bob and June were inwardly motivated to make their marriage work. Joanne and Lew Koch, authors of the book *The Marriage Savers*, write: ''... skills do not a marriage make. If a couple is to prevent conflicting wants from turning into major marital rifts, both husband and wife must have the spirit, the will, the intention to love.''[38]

Bob and June also kept praying even though anger and resentment and frustration would lead them to want to shake their fists at God. At least the lines were kept open, providing that tiny ray of hope which burst into brilliance when the right time came. In prayer they could not only dump all the garbage of their negative feelings but find a safety valve for their bitterness and hate. In other words, they knew how to be perfectly honest with their feelings, telling God at first that they couldn't stand it any longer, that they couldn't care less and, finally, that they wanted to try again. Through it all, they did not break contact with God. He was still the third party to their marriage, the apex of the triangle.

When at long last they made a new start, they also knew where to lay the tribute of their gratitude. In addition, God gave them both the vision and the opportunity to use their experience in helping others who are going through the same deep waters. And in passing it on they are forever consolidating and enhancing their new marriage and the more they give the more they have.

Taking an overview of their story, we can see how they moved from being in a vicious circle of defeat to living a positive cycle of increasing maturity. When Bob was trying to justify his actions by thinking only of his own happiness, it escaped him. When he forgot about that, allowed himself to be broken, even to the depths of personal misery, he was immediately on the road to happiness. Like the wild man who was bound and chained outside and a bundle of conflicts inside Bob and June came to the place where they were seated at Jesus' feet, clothed (with peace and contentment not their own) and in their right mind. When each was inwardly healed, their marriage was made whole.

This is the amazing difference Christ can make in a marriage. In Him a couple can learn how to drive each other sane.

FREE TOGETHER

Many married couples maintain a joint bank account. Both deposit, withdraw, receive the interest, and no record is kept as to who puts how much in or takes out more. It is mutual, practical and convenient, a symbol of oneness.

Other couples think this calls for too much vulnerability. For them it is just too risky to put hard-earned money into another person's hands. "We tried it but the only interest paid was in terms of squabbles, accusations and misunderstandings," said one woman.

How much togetherness is expected in a good marriage? Does it rob one of personal liberty and individuality? Is it foolish to commit yourself so entirely to one person that you don't leave yourself a way out? Many would advise "Don't burn your bridges behind you and always keep your options open!"

Marriage in the "fully together" sense is having a hard time today. "Monogamy?—it's for the birds!" says the well-known movie actress Shirley MacLaine. A man came home from work, burst through the door and shouted, "Darling, I've received a promotion. Do you know what this means? Now we can get a divorce!" Is this the luxury some marrieds crave? For many, it would seem that marriage has turned out to be a one-way ticket to boredom and hostility. Therefore we are not surprised when a social scientist says, "The rising divorce rate is not a catastrophe. It's overdue. People are stepping out into life again to grow as individuals, awakening to their own human potential."[39]

I stood in a local bookstore and looked over their shelf of new publications. Here was one on *How To Survive Divorce*, another, *How to Uncouple Successfully*, and a third, *How To Get Over The Trauma Of Separation Quickly*. There are now divorce greeting cards, and at least one clergyman has designed a special ceremony for "divorce with dignity" to which relatives and friends are invited, just as to a wedding.

Both men and women want more than what traditional marriage seems to offer. What woman wants to be the "chore girl" for the family? Who wants to be tied to meal-getting, working without pay and assuming the role of "second-class citizen" in a so-called man's world? People used to expect marriage to provide safety and security. Now they want their more personal needs and inner potential to be met within the context of a lasting relationship. They look for total fulfillment.

The feminist movement has helped to highlight these rising expectations even though it may have put some husbands on the defensive. A cartoon shows a small boy stamping his foot, looking up and shouting defiantly to his dad, "Stop yelling at me, you're not my mother!" It has even been suggested by some psychologists that there is a direct connection between the male's plummeting prestige and the sharp rise in peptic ulcers among husbands.

Today's woman sees herself as no longer fulfilling the old role of housewife, forever at the beck and call of husband and children. She is moving into the more creative role of companion, and beyond that to the status of equal partner. With this there is a reaching out for sexual freedom and continued romance. Being an equal partner she is claiming equal rights, independent of child-bearing.

Other factors contribute to this new mood. There is a sense of transience in our society, a kind of throw-away mentality, caused in part by the fact that one family in four moves every year. This means adjusting to new jobs and having to make new friends. Roots don't go down very far, so the binding force of community is forever breaking up and being re-formed. The effects of this are bound to spill over into the more intimate community of marriage itself, the prevailing thought being that if nothing lasts why should two persons have to endure a painful relationship?

Looking around for alternatives some people choose communal marriage in which everybody, including the children, belongs to everybody else. Who bothers to sort it all out? Then there is open marriage in which two people may live together but grant each other freedom to have sexual relationships with others without fear of judgement. Or, some couples may elect to live together on the basis of trial marriage, leaving the wedding ceremony as an undiscussed possibility sometime in the dim future. Others get married but sign a renewable contract, "... as long as we both shall love," or "I, John, take thee, Mary, for the next five years."

One man, divorced and lonely after twenty-six years and being unwilling to marry again, decided to "hire" a wife. He put an ad in the paper and had scores of replies. From these he chose one, paid her a monthly salary with guaranteed duties, days off and vacation time. He said he found brief affairs with intermittent periods of loneliness too much to bear, so he struck on the idea of hiring a wife he could shed without government interference. He said he wanted to go solo, "unsuppressed by togetherness and by loved possessed."[40]

Proponents of these alternatives keep telling us they are "more honest." These options provide a kind of insulation against the pain and general messiness of possible divorce. The underlying idea is don't expect too much of marriage and you won't be disappointed. Anticipate failure. If the coupling works out, well and good, but if not, you simply shrug your shoulders and move on to somebody else.

Of one thing we can be sure and that is there is nothing new about serial coupling. In the best circles of ancient Rome it was considered unfashionable and indeed uncouth to stay married to the same spouse too long. Among the well-known Romans, Ovid was married three times, Caesar four times and Pompey five times. A woman's age was not counted in years but she was said to be three or four or six husbands old.

We are beginning to appreciate some of the positive values of the sexual revolution. At first we didn't know what to do with it and feared it may have been spelling the end of the family. But now that the windows have been opened and fresh breezes of communication are blowing, we are finding that people are more likely to get married because they really want to, rather than for social or economic or family reasons alone. They are demanding more and getting more of marriage. They are entering with higher expectations, finding their deepest emotional needs fulfilled and discovering the finer joys of true partnership.

At the same time we are beginning to sort out and discard a few of the more bizarre experiments as well as reversing many ideas that were latched onto so eagerly. In the early seventies, Nena and George O'Neill wrote a bestselling book entitled *Open Marriage*. Their main idea was that if it feels good, do it. Any couple who had "mature love" could, at the same time, carry on an outside relationship. This would presumably expand them toward loving and enjoying others and then bring their experience back into their marriage without jealousy. It all sounded beautiful.

There was only one problem, — it didn't work! Now they have

written another book, *The Marriage Premise*, in which they say, "Sexual fidelity is not just a vow in marriage or a religious belief, but a need associated with our deepest emotions and our quest for security."[41] They found that many couples were returning, battle-scarred and weary, to the belief in a commitment to one person only.

With a whole panoply of sexual possibilities spread out before them, many couples are consequently choosing to remain in the confines of monogamous marriage. "Swinging's out," they say, "fidelity is in, and faithfulness is back in style."

We are living in a backlash against a libertinism that posed as emancipation. People who in the '60s said, "We don't need that piece of paper called a marriage certificate just to have sex," have found through much bitterness that sex outside of marriage is a lonely affair, that living together without vows leads to insecurity and that the real purpose of marriage is not sex but the lasting companionship which they desperately sought but could not find.

A professor of sociology from Columbia University says, "No political society has ever survived without its nuclear family intact."[42] Another says, "People have burnt themselves out chewing on the cob of the liberal. After 15 years what has he produced? A life that is full of barnyard morality."[43] A psychologist says, "The promiscuity concept is dying out . . . . People are talking about fidelity. It's a revolution against loneliness."[44] Perhaps for the first time in history more people may be getting married just for love. Perhaps our whole society has been like the prodigal son in the far country. We've had it, and now we want to go home. A young man put it, "I used to think my parents were stuffy, now I know they achieved the highest kind of happiness."

This basic misunderstanding is typified in the exasperated student of music who believed that the only reason for his poor performance was his instrument. In marriage, freedom and harmony are achieved not by changing partners but in discovering and developing the unrealized potential within the present relationship.

A good marriage is not so much a state as a journey. Where non-committed couples find boredom overtaking them, others discover the beginning of an exciting adventure. And where many ask, "Is this all there is?" and want out, others find new possibilities by going in more deeply. This is a synergism. Two people who have committed their whole lives for their whole future to one another can bring into being something much more than the sum of even their highest individual potentials.

The old wording in the marriage service was, "I plight thee my troth," which means, "I pledge you my faith." In other words, "I believe you; I put my trust in you. When you tell me you love me I think you really mean it." So the basis of Christian marriage is not love so much as it is faith.

This total commitment in marriage is risky and may look like a foolish business. It seems against all common sense to hand over your happiness and your future to the keeping of the person you love at the moment, but who at the same time is a separate individual and remains always, in some sense, a stranger. Yet this act of faith can unlock in each lover new powers of compassion, endurance, generosity, joy, passion, fidelity and hope that no one could have guessed were there.

Our greatest human gifts come to the surface only when two people are thus prepared to gamble everything in each other. One husband who made this discovery put the following classified ad in the daily paper: "Because today marks 15 years that she has been my bride and because she has given me four wonderful children and has been most helpful to keep my home a sanctuary in this confused and troubled world, I am happy to declare that I am responsible for all debts incurred by my wife, Elizabeth."

"You are heirs together of the grace of life," the Bible says (I Peter 3:7). This is like having a joint bank account in which each puts in more than is taken out as the balance grows in terms of love, security, personal fulfillment and growing satisfaction.

One couple who illustrate this are Alva and Gunnar Byrdal of Sweden. He is a Nobel Prize-winning economist, an international social critic and famous author. His wife is a diplomat and antiwar activist. A member of the UN, she has worked for UNESCO, became Sweden's ambassador to India in 1955 and has recently also been awarded a Nobel Peace Prize.

In their busy, globe-trotting lives they are often apart for weeks and months. "We're like consort battleships," says Alva, and while appreciating family and friends, she continues, "we enjoy talking together more than anything else."

Gunnar adds, "People don't realize the great happiness there is in living to be very old and together all the time. The older we get the closer we are!"[45]

My guess is that every couple unconsciously desires what the Myrdal's have achieved. A bride-to-be chooses a certain design of silverware because it is called, "Eternally Yours." A song says, "I'm gonna lock my heart and throw away the key." A Hollywood starlet, about to take her fifth husband said, "This time it's going to be for keeps." These people speak for all of us.

A ship went down in the Caribbean in 1641. Recently divers brought up a gold ring with the inscription, "Be true in heart though far apart." Fascinating! Some sailor, far from the one who loved him, was held to fidelity, exclusiveness and permanence. These are not new or old virtues but fixtures of our human nature in every generation.

When Anna and I were married I wanted our rings to be more than ordinary, so we began to search for a meaningful inscription. One day we found it, and trembling with excitement, asked the jeweller to inscribe the verse, "Magnify the Lord with me and let us exalt His name together" (Psalm 34:3). The word "together" captured my imagination and we have tried to make it the working pattern of our relationship. This is "our verse" from Scripture and it binds us together, holding us to our calling under God.

To keep our relationship fresh and growing we are learning how to massage each other's psyches as well as backs, giving that tender, healing touch which reflects years of growing together. It is a joyful journey and an exciting adventure in which we are both being continually reshaped. As God's love is accepted into ours, the possibilities for our loving each other seem limitless.

A "joint account" marriage moves from the early stages of excitement in setting up house into the responsibilities of raising a family, on to coping with personality conflict, through the frustrations of seeing children grow and choose friends and mates of their own, then toward a deeper companionship marked by a growing sense of personal fulfillment and maturing romance. It's an exciting journey. As one woman put it, "Ours has been a strange and wonderful relationship. I'm strange and he's wonderful."

Yet Anna and I have sensed danger in all this. It could turn into idolatry. Marriage can be divine but it is not God. Exalting the idea of happiness is one way to miss it, because while marriage is great, it isn't everything. Only God is everything, and His spirit in any marriage can make it wonderful.

A well-known Hollywood actor and actress were married twice. The first time they took their vows before a judge and after four years agreed to call it quits. "There was nothing really wrong with our marriage," she said, "but no amount of good behavior on our part seemed to put into it the elements we had dreamed of."

Then one night between production schedules, they managed to have a talk. He said, "If I ever get married again I'll be a better husband."

"Sure," she replied, "and when I get married again I'll be a better wife."

They sat looking at each other. He ventured, "I suppose I'll never meet anybody perfect."

She said the same, then added, "Well, if we're both going to be a better spouse it seems a shame to give someone else the benefit of our experience. We could try it on each other."

They did. But it still was not all that they expected it to be until they turned to God. She says, "I took three months to prepare myself spiritually for our second marriage. The covenant we had made before man was now made before God. I was converting a legal agreement into a sacrament."

Then a verse of Scripture became meaningful to them: "Except the Lord build the house they labour in vain that build it" (Psalm 27:1). She adds, "Things began to change between my husband and me. I sensed a new nearness, a deeper warmth, as if we were always holding hands. We found that spiritual grace was the wedding gift God gave us—not bath towels but peace of heart, patience, understanding and love. Grace swept into our lives."[46]

To their surprise they discovered new freedom, freedom in maturity, freedom in togetherness . . . with God. This is available to any couple who dare choose to become "heirs together of the grace of life."

WHEN FAMILIARITY BREEDS CONTENTMENT

Of the few things my father had to say to me about marriage I remember one aphorism especially: "Many fellows fall in love with a dimple and then make the mistake of marrying the whole girl."

That came home to me when I read these comments by C.S. Lewis: ". . . we say of a lustful man prowling the streets, that he 'wants a woman.' Strictly speaking, a woman is just what he does not want. He wants a pleasure for which a woman happens to be the necessary piece of apparatus. How much he cares about the woman . . . may be gauged by his attitude to her five minutes after fruition (one does not keep the carton after one has smoked the cigarettes)."[46]

Marriage is for persons who are willing to give as much as possible of themselves toward the fulfillment of each other. Anything short of that is a continued source of inner frustration.

A woman writes: "In real life I never believed I would marry. Lesser women could get married, have children, be dependent, if they must. I was too confident, self-assured, independent to want or need marriage.

"I looked around at the marriages I knew and I didn't like what I saw. People locked together, bound by a probably long-outdated contract. It seemed to me that people who got married stopped trying after a while. They took each other for granted. They didn't flirt or tease or do any of the sexy things people who lived together did. And of course children were the crippling blow to any relationship. Death in life. That's what marriage seemed to me.

"Then I looked around at couples who were living together and I liked what I saw. There was life, a sense of freedom, they were together because they wanted to be and it looked as if they had more fun. They weren't always talking about mortgages and babysitters and money and the future. They were living for now. They had excitement, romance, adventure. They travelled, went out to dinner a lot, took off when they felt like it.

"Too, the woman was her own person: working, earning her own money. She had her own name, her own indentity, not just folded in with his name and forgotten. In my mind, living together made people happy and marriage made them sad. So I had several live-in persons.

"I can't say exactly or give a time or place when I suddenly decided I wanted to get married. The first thing I remember is being angry that he didn't seem to want to get married. Why wasn't he down on his knees begging me to change my mind? After all, he couldn't really love me if he didn't want to marry me. It never occurred to me to turn that around. Could I really love him if I didn't want to marry him?

"I wanted to be not only loved but cherished. You don't cherish your live-in girlfriend. You only cherish your wife. Then I got thinking about the future. One day I felt free not being married. The next day I was thinking of the song which goes: 'Freedom's just another word for nothin' left to lose.'

"We always bought things separately so that if we were to break up there would be no hassle. We didn't own a toothpick together. But I didn't like predicating every move of the relationship on the possibility of separation. Now where I felt free before, I felt insecure. I didn't want to fight or argue because if I got mad enough I could just leave. Or he could. That put restrictions on communication. Finally I realized I wanted to get married.

"Marriage is definition of who and what you are together. It puts a frame around the relationship. There is a sense of freedom now that there wasn't before. Living together took up so much emotional energy. Now I felt liberated to expend my emotional energy on other things like loving completely. It is so relaxing to be married.

"The weekend we got married I was so happy that I felt as if someone had poured a whole bottle of Golden Mountain honey over the world; everything was so soft and warm and mellow and romantic. It was perfect, as I had always dreamed it was going to be."[48]

Well, here is one person who discovered that "a girl is more than a dimple," that only marriage in terms of life-long commitment can satisfy the whole person, meeting needs of body, mind, spirit, emotions. Sometimes it takes years for the deeper needs to come to the surface. For a long time they might be ignored or denied, but sooner or later they begin to scream for attention. And that's when marriage will either rise or fall.

One marriage counsellor says, "Man must have long-term intimate relationships. He must have a secure and permanent base in life. He must believe that there is someone who will accept and continue to care. You can't accomplish that with someone who has a casual or temporary commitment. As long as man craves for permanence in his life he will seek marriage."[49]

A young couple get married. Let's assume that they make a good sexual adjustment—and for a while that seems to be everything. In fact, they want each other so much that nothing else really matters. They could live in a single room somewhere and need nothing more than a tea kettle. Furniture? What's wrong with orange crates? But soon these conditions begin to look rather grim and they want to embellish their marriage with some "nice things."

Some deeper personal needs begin to be felt. In fact, as time goes on they will probably sense a whole bundle of needs in themselves. They crave adventure. Building a nest is great but that's only half the picture. Life is a journey and the instincts to grow and learn and explore must also be met. They need friends, so that knowing others they can have a deeper understanding of themselves. They need books to lift their vision to a world wider than their own limited and private one. Life requires drama.

By now they may sense a need to be affirmed. Through all the necessary adjustments of learning to get along together, the business of mutual affirmation can easily be forgotten, even to the point of feeling rejected by one's mate. Then a couple learns that the fabric of self-esteem is easily torn and needs to be perpetually repaired. As one man stated, "It's one thing to be wanted between the sheets and quite another thing to be cherished in the daily round."

Then there is the need for emotional security. This is hardly evident at the beginning of marriage, being obscured by the exuberance of romantic embrace. Here we should distinguish between adultery and infidelity. Adultery is an incident, ugly and destructive and painful. But infidelity is quitting, refusing to continue to bring out the best that is the other. Infidelity dashes hope because a person is no longer willing to try. One writer says, "Fidelity is the permanent, public, solemn and an irrevocable commitment to dedicate one's life to bring out the best in one's partner and in oneself." Fidelity assumes that the original evaluation of the other was a correct one. It may have been limited and incomplete yet an adequate base from which to expand and grow. A woman summed it up when asked what she saw in the man she married. She replied, "I said to myself, he's the person

I want to grow old with."

The need emerges to have somebody to talk to, to be heard and understood. A woman who had come through the traumatic experience of the breakup of her marriage said: "In these four years I have often been alone but never lonely. But in twenty-five years of marriage it was ghastly how alone I was with no warmth or communication." Perhaps one of the greatest gifts we can give in marriage is listening, the very basis of companionship and communication. If the basic needs are seen to be only bed and board, then slowly but surely there grows a profound loneliness that is deeper and more devastating psychologically than living alone. So many couples are lacking in this area that it is almost assumed there is loneliness and tension. "Does your wife understand you?" asked one man of another.

"Of course not," was the immediate response.

A woman said, "I long for my husband to communicate that he loves me in non-sexual ways." She was all for sex, but longed to hear some affectionate words without all the overtones of the sexual embrace.

A recent study by a New York psychiatrist, *Beyond The Male Myth*, indicates that men are less interested in sexual pleasure than in love and companionship. Seventy percent of all men said that marriage was the ideal. "We ask questions about sex and get answers that discuss the need to change, to develop, to build and grow, from men who do not want to confront this life task alone."[50] The author said, "Today, men don't marry for regular sex or primarily for children. Rather, men are looking at women more as companions."[51]

A young widow says, "The one thing I miss is the quiet part of our lives. I miss the times when we would both be busy at the same time, close by one another, just looking up once in a while to see what the other was doing. In those quiet times nothing earth-shaking happened. There was just the comfort of knowing we both cared, that we were not alone. It was someone to be quiet with."[52]

Not many couples think of these things when they get married. They want action, dancing, skiing, partying. But while these are going on something deeper is emerging, just the plain joy of being in each other's company and learning to cherish the quiet times.

There is also the need for fun and laughter and light-heartedness. Teasing, jostling, joking and even arguing without acrimony fulfills the instinct for playful give-and-take which helps to strengthen the bonds of togetherness.

All of these and many more form a bundle of desires inherent in our nature which we expect marriage to fulfill.

When marriage is emotionally satisfying, intellectually stimulating and spiritually nourishing it sets two people free to become all that they potentially are. The point is not that they ever arrive but that they experience joy in knowing that they are on the way. Such a marriage is "liberated."

This doesn't happen all at once and even a liberated marriage doesn't move ahead evenly on all fronts. There are spurts and starts, recessions and many stops along the way. Anna and I have found that our relationship progresses in cycles. The same basic questions confront us at every time of crisis: Do we really love each other? Is our marriage growing stale? Are we allowing each other to be free? Are we feeding and being adequately fed all the ingredients necessary for a healthy relationship? Is our marriage going anywhere? And most of all, at this particular stage of life, are we finding contentment? Facing up to these questions as they are thrown at us by living and working things out together is a healthy exercise, helping us to keep fresh with a sense of daily newness in our marriage. It keeps romance alive.

Always lurking in the background is the sinister temptation to withdraw into oneself rather than to be present to one another. This can lead to frustration and perhaps even to physical illness.

I'm a firm believer that husbands and wives can bring on sickness to one another, victimizing each other unconsciously, with no intention to do so. Spouses must share a good part of the blame for each other's ailments. A recent study of patients with perforated ulcers of the stomach and duodenum showed that most of them had been trying to resolve some type of emotional crisis. What marriage doesn't produce emotional crises from time to time?

Dr. Hans Selye says that many common diseases are largely due to stress and that unhappy persons seem to show a lessened resistance to cancer. Of 237 men who had survived their first heart attack, he found the overwhelming majority had been consistently downgraded by nagging wives.[53] Another authority says, "When you hit a person's self-esteem, the reaction can lead to physical illness," and gives an example how streptococcus bacteria multiply in the throat during emotional stress. It would seem that any prolonged emotional strain tends to reduce the body's immunity to disease. All of this would strongly suggest that good health and a liberated marriage are bound inextricably together. So a couple who have found contentment help keep each other healthy.

No one form of marriage is the complete answer to freedom and contentment. There is tremendous reaction today against the traditional form of the nuclear family: father being the authority figure and bringing home the paycheck, mother looking after the meals and the house, children trained to be obedient and respectful in all things. The Bible comes in for criticism here—especially Paul who would seem to have advocated that women should be submissive to their husbands even as husbands must love their wives (Ephesians 5:22-33). That doesn't harmonize with today's mood of liberation. Perhaps rightly so!

When we see the passage in its total context, however, we realize that Paul is calling for mutual submission and that the admonition for husbands to love their wives creates the very liberty that women desire most. Moreover, it is the kind of love that Christ has for his Church, not that which dominates but that which gives its life. It leads not to control but to crucifixion.

Anna and I have struggled with this and have come to appreciate the subtler meanings of mutual submission. The other day I came in from doing the family banking for the month and tried to share with Anna some of the higher intricacies of the financial world: interest rates, loan values, mortgage reduction, et cetera, with overtones in my voice of, "I wish you'd do this once in a while," or "I hope you don't think I'm grabbing this department." But she responded with, "Well, I'm glad you do this for us," and continued to concentrate on her project of the moment. Some persons might look on this and say it is intolerable, thinking that a husband and wife should share everything on an equal basis and have a mutual hand in all the affairs of the household.

To me it is not a matter of there being a right way or wrong, as long as the pattern adopted is mutually acceptable. Of course marriage should be democratic, but any arrangement of doing the necessary chores can succeed or fail depending on the interests and attitudes of each person and whether or not each is comfortable with the way these things are done. Being sensitive to each other's desires and flexible to change in order to meet those desires are the fundamental factors that can set a couple free in this area.

I'm an unabashed fan of marriage. It's stomping around each other in the kitchen, stopping for an occasional squeeze. It's cuddling at night, knowing that no matter how badly you've blown it during the course of the day there is always that someone who regards you as special. I think I have found where real peace and contentment lie. Anna and I have shared too many good times, heartaches and struggles together to not want to go forward in the best adventure of all, continually experiencing each other as changing persons. This is the familiarity that breeds contentment and the kind of marriage that sets each partner free.

AND IT KEEPS GETTING BETTER

A husband writes: "Today, after 26 years of marriage, I am more sensitive to the thrill of her presence than I have ever been. When I meet her unexpectedly in a crowd, it is like a glad little song rising up somewhere inside me. When I catch her eye in public it is as though she were hanging out a sign with the exact word of inspiration I need right then. When I drive home in the evening, I must consciously guard the foot-pedal lest I drive too fast as I approach the house where she waits for me. I still count it the day's biggest thrill when she comes hurrying from where ever she is to greet me. And as I look down the road ahead, I see an elderly man and woman going into the sunset hand in hand. I know in my heart that the end will be better by far than the beginning."[54]

What is this? Some impractical idealist writing out of his private dream world? Is he some weak-kneed, hen-pecked husband of an overbearing wife writing out of his fear of a verbal lashing if he honestly spoke his mind? Perhaps he isn't telling the whole truth, or else he forgets the quarrels, tensions, bickerings, threats, and "drag'em out, knock'em down" fights they've had through the years.

Wrong! This is one party of a secure marriage in which two persons have matured through plenty of difficulties, who regard the stages of the passing years as growing points, each one with its own intriguing challenge, and who are beginning to reap the benefits of sticking it out through thick and thin. What began in the violence of wild love is now in the calm waters of peaceful partnership. The passionate flame has been transformed into the warm afterglow of companionable love. Like two trees that at first competed for soil and sunshine but now stand straight and strong because their roots and thousands of rootlets are intertwined, so the years have integrated these two lives into a marvelous unity of interdependence. Someone

93

described a marriage like this: when one person cries the other tastes salt.

Later years tend to reveal what's been going on over the decades. Young people may manage to hide their inner attitudes, suppress their anger, ignore their feelings of loneliness, ride over their emotional needs. They can go on for a long time through busy years pretending that these dark shadows are not there and believing they will eventually go away.

But as Jesus said, "There is nothing hidden that shall not be revealed" (Luke 12:2). In one form or another it all comes out. Cynicism, boredom, bitterness, and a variety of physical ailments tell the tale for all the world to know. Many psychological and emotional problems surface as old age approaches, but so also do the joys, achievements, tenderness and the fact that two people have managed to keep alive that vital force, the fires of love that brought them together in the first place.

Of one couple it was said, "Theirs was a teenage love that has lasted seventy years." Julius and Jenny emigrated from Russia near the turn of the century. They worked together for all their years in a joint business enterprise. Now, due to a series of strokes, Jennie is in a centre for geriatric care, but Julius visits her every afternoon, seven days a week, and sings songs to her in their native language. You can tell by the way her face lights up that every song is of love.

Couples like this can be found in almost any community. They've worked at their marriage, building it not on the shaky foundation of teenage romance. Their well-earned love is closer to being the fond smile which an old man with snow-white hair, a little hard of hearing, reading the newspaper through a magnifying glass casts upon his wife who wears a shapeless dress, sandals to ease her aching arches and whose knuckles are gnarled by arthritis. In a little while they will totter off to take their nap. Then she will cook supper, not a very good supper, and they may watch television, knowing exactly what the other is thinking, until it is time for bed. Through the night they will snore in rhythm, each resting content because the other is there. They are in love! They have always been in love. They have survived everything life could throw at them, even their own failures. They may even be seen holding hands.

They have long since learned that the tide of happiness in any marriage ebbs and flows. Ecstatically happy at times, excruciatingly wounded at other times, a mixture of good and bad in between, they no longer despair when tensions threaten to drive them apart nor are they surprised when personal idiosyncrasies conflict. They've been over the road several times.

They are familiar with the meanings of certain innuendoes in communication. They know when their mate is tired or especially vulnerable to suggestion, just as they can sense a festive mood coming on. They know when small arguments could escalate into major proportions, but also what small gestures can relieve tension and create peace. In short, they know that it is not a matter of having or not having "a happy marriage." Their marriage at any given moment is only what they themselves are willing to make it, that it doesn't just "turn out" this way or that, but is the result of their own individual investment in making it turn out right.

They know that a good marriage doesn't just happen. And when things are not perfect they are honest enough to admit that it can't be blamed on chemistry, upbringing, separate interests or each other. In learning to see their own foibles and to laugh at their own peculiarities they have found freedom through the years to change and grow into more mature, responsible personalities.

They have found freedom from the tyranny of the trivial. All those little adjustments that must be made in early marriage: steak well done or rare, window open or closed, toothpaste tube squeezed from bottom or top—such seemingly insignificant items can add up to life of continual irritation or of light-hearted humour. It all depends on the willingness of each person to rise to the uniqueness of the other. The choice is between friction or freedom, disappointment or discovery.

I am reminded of the young man who was engaged to be married and bought his girl a ring. Since he was a struggling student and had very little money the diamond was rather small. When the time came to give the ring to her he was very apologetic and said, "I'm sorry it's such a small stone."

But she immediately replied, "It's as big as we choose to make it." Right on!

The Bible says, "Outdo one another in showing honor" (Romans 12:10). If this desire is present, then, instead of competing with one another for ascendency, a couple may compete in giving in, in pleasing each other, in finding delight by making life comfortable for the loved one. They rise above the trivial.

The trivial can also dominate conversation. When a couple reach the stage of life when the children are gone they may sit across from each other at the table and stare into space, not daring to look at each other for fear of havng to admit they are really strangers who have nothing important to say. For years their conversation has been only about the little things that make up daily existence. They have seldom talked seriously about life, about values, about ultimates. Now they sense an emptiness which shows itself in boredom. They tolerate each other through multiple diversions and shallow entertainment. They are trapped in a cycle of days and nights that repeat themselves with little meaning or goal.

A woman of sixty-eight looked at her husband one day and said, "Honey, what are we alive for anyway?"

He wondered what had come over her. All he wanted to know was what was the TV special that Saturday night and if they had an adequate supply of beer on hand. After a moment's reflection he turned and said, "Let's change the subject."

"That's the trouble," she objected, "you always want to change the subject."

Only when two people are caught up in something much bigger than themselves, seeing their lives as fulfilling a divine plan, always ready to examine life's basic assumptions, who worship and pray and sing and serve together, can they escape the tyranny of the trivial. They have something to talk about because they know what they are alive for.

Without this a couple can be victimized by the craze for pleasure, which has been vividly described in these words: "Across the border there must be still stronger wine, across the ocean there must be still madder music, across the continent there must be still greater exhilaration, across the city there must be still wilder thrills. All you gotta do is keep moving, moving, moving and faster, faster, faster, away from the restrictions of society and toward the realm of sheer delight to which no two people have ever travelled before." Surely this kind of life is like a monster. The more you feed it the hungrier it gets.

Anna and I are both readers, so our house is stacked with books. One room is filled with my books and another with hers. Then we have several shelves of volumes that belong to the whole family. We each have books by our bedside. Not able to find a reference in my section, I go to hers—and vice versa. Almost every night for upwards to an hour we read in bed, privately, whatever book may intrigue each of us at the moment. It is a beautifully restful time. Filled with my own thoughts, Anna is also filled with hers. We are individually ourselves yet one at a very deep level, only interrupting each other to ask the meaning of a word or to share a good story or perhaps a funny incident that is too good to keep to ourselves.

Most nights we agree about when the time has come to turn off the light. Sleep then overtakes us quickly as we rest in the knowledge that while we may not have a clue about what the other person has been reading, we are of one mind just the same.

As years pass couples may also be threatened by the tyranny of the calendar. I have heard it said that a person is not ''old'' until the candles of his birthday cake set off the smoke alarm! Yet many have long since surrendered to our youth-oriented culture and to them the horror of horrors is to appear old. Millions of dollars are spent to erase the telltale traces of aging: grey hair, crow's feet wrinkles around the eyes and those ''horrid little brown spots'' on the hands.

Some think they are old at forty and at sixty-five definitely on the scrap heap. Old age, to many, spells a physical decline with visions of arthritic fingers and failing eyesight. There is also the fear of having to be tolerated by eager young people whose aggressive enthusiasm infers that oldsters are somehow in the way.

That picture, however, is quickly changing. More and more people today are approaching middle age with a sense of release from family responsibilities. They are taking new part-time jobs, going back to school, learning new skills, travelling to exciting places or applying past experience to voluntary service which is both self-fulfilling and a stimulus to community. Life for many begins at sixty, or even seventy. One man at eighty said he thought it was time to marry and settle down.

In *Through The Looking Glass* Alice said, ''You know, one cannot help growing old.''

''One can't, perhaps,'' said Humpty Dumpty, ''but two can.''

In a nutshell! Two can do a lot of things for each other and there are many ''youngsters'' who have kept each other from growing old through fifty years of marriage.

E. Stanley Jones wrote, ''I am fifty-eight and I love it—I wouldn't be twenty-eight for anything: fifty-eight is too interesting and too full and too adventurous! I am simply tingling with interests. And in the midst of these interests there is a calm and an undisturbable poise I did not have when younger. Life begins at fifty-eight.''[55]

A Quaker nurse said, ''Beyond fifty, after my change in life, I found a freedom and a calm, and an interest in people as people, and not merely as sex beings.'' She found new liberty.

Nobody can say for sure when old age begins. What we do know is that after sixty-five some people find not only a new burst of energy but a whole new world of interest and excitement. They discover new powers in themselves; the added decades are packed with satisfactions, interests and possibilities more exhilarating than those of any previous period.

At age one hundred, Grandma Moses was painting. At ninety-four, Bertrand Russell was active in international peace drives. At ninety-two Bernard Shaw wrote a new play. At eighty-nine, Albert Schweitzer headed a hospital in Africa. At eighty-seven, Konrad Adenauer was Chancellor of Germany. At eighty, Fred Astaire took to himself a new wife. At eighty, George Burns won an Academy Award and at eighty-four is still acting and singing in TV specials. When is ''old?''

This tyranny of the calendar also raised the fear of loss of sexual powers. Research into this question, however, reveals the fact that given the conditions of reasonably good health, elderly persons continue to be sexually active even into their seventh, eighth and ninth decades. Young people do not have a monopoly on sexuality. Nor does the sexual bond necessarily have to recede after middle age. In this regard we have to jettison a whole collection of dusty, moth-eaten ideas we have inherited from generations past. For while lovemaking may be neither so frequent nor so ardent as it used to be, it can be more rewarding and even more enjoyable.

In this regard a couple must learn how to fully relax realizing that it is not important to ''perform'' to some preconceived level of excellence. Every marriage is different in these matters, unique as to needs, desires and lasting satisfactions. Each person in a marriage needs to feel loved, and age certainly does not lessen that need; on the contrary, it increases. There is the comfort of physical nearness, the pleasure of companionship, the reward of emotional intimacy and of shared joys. Occasionally there may be difficulty in attaining what we formerly might have thought was the climax of the sexual act. But if a couple really love each other, this need not bother them or inhibit their love. Other ways of expressing endearment will not only suffice but will have infinitely more joy than in earlier years.

A man said, ''The first time I found I was impotent I felt devastated and denigrated as a man, embarrassed and filled with fears. But right then my wife said, 'Dear, it doesn't matter. I know you love me and I love you.' When I heard that I was relieved, reassured and restored. I felt like a man again and a lover."

One discovery, particularly of older years, is that the most important sex organ is the mind. Images, fantasies, anticipation and thoughts of tender love can make all the difference. And, speaking from experience, the more holy and prayerful the thoughts, the more beautiful is the embrace. One specialist in this subject says that there are two types of male preparedness, the one physical and the other cerebral—and these must work together.[56] In later years, because of anxiety the physical may gain great importance. But my experience is that it needn't end there. There is a deeper dimension still. Spirituality, prayer and unity in Christ can stimulate both the physical and the cerebral and bring a depth to the sexual embrace that is nothing short of pure ecstasy.

We can go far beyond the secular approach of a man like Kinsey, whose investigators said, "Good health, sufficient exercise and plenty of sleep remain the most effective of the aphrodisiacs known to man."[57] To be one in spirit, to feel God's love pervading our human love, to enter into the sex act with a profound sense of gratitude to God for life, for love, for each other, for children, grandchildren and the home is to put the whole matter within the context of eternal love, which makes it truly "heavenly." This is a key to freedom that can never come from the scientist *per se*, nor from research, nor from reams of statistics. And whenever or wherever there seems to be a decrease in sexual activity as later years approach, it is more than compensated for by a vastly increased degree of affection.

With this spiritual key, sex is allowed to take its rightful place both in younger couples and older. It is not God and is not to be idolized. It reaches its highest potential when it is not the be-all and end-all of marriage. It fulfills itself when it is not an absolute goal, rather, a way to express affection, companionship, shared feelings and soul communication. It is most satisfying when it is looked on as a gift from God, intended primarily for fellowship at the most profound depths.

Sexuality is then recognized as being far more than physical intercourse. It is appreciation, grace, a touch of eternity. Marriage grows into something much more wonderful than erotic union. The physical may play a more minor role, but that in no way stops the flow of affection or the experience of oneness that is so much a treasure in older years.

So to married folk who are concerned with what the future holds in store for them especially in the latter half of life, the good news is that it can get better and better. One of God's most precious promises is just this:

Even to your old age I am He,
and to grey hairs I will carry you.
I have made, and I will bear;
I will carry and will save.

Isaiah 46:4

Yes, there is marvelous freedom in later years and there are lots of folks who can prove it. The poet was right:

Grow old along with me!
The best is yet to be,
The last of life, for which the first was made:
Our times are in His hand
Who saith, 'A whole I planned,'
Youth shows but half; trust God: see all,
      nor be afraid.

Robert Browning

SO WHO'S PERFECT?

The last chapter of a prominent book is entitled, "The Displaced Preface." In the same way I feel this closing word could very well have been at the beginning, but in either place it summarizes the theme and purpose of my writing.

What's a perfect marriage? Has anybody ever seen one? Is there such a creature as a perfect wife or a perfect husband? If so, would you want to live with them? More to the point, would they want to live with you? The other day I heard this: "If your wife doesn't treat you as you deserve—be thankful."

We are often quick to excuse our conduct by tossing off the remark, "Well, what do you expect? Nobody's perfect." The fact is, that although we tend to think of ourselves as a cut or two above others, we can give this idea a quick flip over and conclude that while others have no right to expect perfection from us, somehow we have a right to be disappointed if we don't find perfection in them.

One December a man came home with one of the new-fangled, synthetic Christmas trees. Setting it up in the corner it stood there with its sprayed-on glacial blue paint and its Aqua Velva scent. At first he thought he could use this tree year after year since the needles would never fall to the carpet, but he soon came to despise it. One day in a burst of indignation, he threw it out. He said, "It was so perfect it was unreal. It didn't even have a bad side to be turned to the wall."

The perfect tree was not perfect because it was plastic. So some marriage partners try to be plastic-perfect. They do everything exactly right. They are neat and tidy and always on time. They don't get ruffled, lose their temper, waste money or over-do the vegetables. But the home is hell, until one party screams, "I want to be married to a real person—not a machine."

In the cartoon "Peanuts," Lucy says, "Charlie Brown, some-

101

times I could hug you and sometimes you bug me.''

He lets that sink in for a moment and replies, ''Well, that's what I am, huggable and buggable.''

That's what we all are and that's what makes us genuine persons and what constitutes a real marriage. What couple would not agree with Pogo: ''We have faults we've hardly used yet''?

A woman who had been brought up on the perfectionist concept tried to achieve it in everything. But her life came under such strain and stress that she broke under the weight. Her marriage dissolved, her profession rejected her and she became an alcoholic, convinced that she was a total failure. ''I worked hard,'' she said, ''to build my credentials as a deserving member of society.'' Then some friends took her to a Christian meeting. There she heard deep sharing of hurts, weaknesses, failures and sins. But along with that there was supportiveness, love and hope. She was hearing good news and began to think that, just possibly, there was still some hope for her.

As a child, she had been a church-goer and learned Bible stories. But she had never truly heard the Gospel. Christianity, to her, was making yourself acceptable to God, another reason to strive even harder for perfection. But now she heard something different—that we are made perfect in God's perfection through Christ. It is His gift and not our attainment. In time, as this revolutionary idea took root, she was healed and changed and began a new life.[58]

Christian perfection saves us from perfectionism. The Bible says, ''God will make you perfect'' (I Peter 5:10, T.E.V.). God can also make a marriage perfect when the partners can accept through His love the imperfections of each other. A man was complaining about his wife when his friend reminded him, ''But you took her for better or for worse.''

''Yes,'' was his reply, ''but she's worse than I took her for!''. We all are! A friend of mine says, ''Difficult husbands are the only kind God makes.'' The same could be said of wives. A woman said, ''There are just two reasons why our marriage is not perfect and I'm one of them.'' She was being realistic and human. Yet when we choose to see our spouses through the eyes of God's grace they turn out to be better than we took them for. The gap between what they are and what we might wish they would become is closed. That bone of contention is gone and the release is marvelous.

102

Perfectionism, then, is not in ourselves but always in the eyes of the beholder. One Christian leader said, ''Our aim in marriage is to hold above the head of the other person a crown of creative expectation which all the rest of his life he will be trying to grow tall enough to wear.'' That crown is our worth in the eyes of a lover. That is what makes a boy a perfect hockey player, in the eyes of his mother; a son who graduates from school, a genius in the eyes of his father; a mother, the best cook in the world in the eyes of a daughter; a husband, the world's most handsome man in the eyes of his wife; a wife, the world's beauty queen in the eyes of a husband. A man said to his wife, ''I'm not what I think I am and I'm not what you think I am, I'm what I think you think I am.'' Our imperfections are overcome by grace, which is undeserved love.

Most people are familiar with the old song, ''Believe Me If All Those Endearing Young Charms.'' It was written by an Irish poet, Thomas Moore, who had just been married to a very beautiful woman. He was called away on a business trip and on his return was met at the door, not by his bride, but by the family doctor.

''Your wife is upstairs,'' said the doctor, ''but she has asked that you do not come up.''

Then Moore learned the terrible truth: his wife had contracted smallpox, leaving her once flawless skin pocked and scarred. She had taken one look at her reflection in the mirror and commanded that the shutters be drawn and that her husband never see her again.

But Moore would not listen. He ran upstairs and threw open the door of his wife's room. It was black as night. He felt for a lamp. A startled cry came from his wife. ''No, don't light the lamps!'' Moore hesitated. ''Go,'' she begged. ''Please go! This is the greatest gift I can give you now.''

Moore did go. He went down to his study where he sat up most of the night, prayerfully writing, not a poem but a song, though he had never written music before. The next morning as the sun was up he returned to his wife's room, quietly asking, ''Are you awake?''

''I am,'' came her voice, ''but you must not ask to see me, you must not press me, Thomas.''

''I will sing to you, then,'' he answered. And so he sang those words that still live today:

Believe me, if all those endearing young charms,
Which I gaze on so fondly today,
Were to change by tomorrow, and flee in my arms,

103

Like fairy gifts fading away,
Thou would still be adored, as this moment thou art . . .
Let thy loveliness fade as it will,
And around the dear ruin each wish of my heart
Would entwine itself verdantly still . . .

The song ended. Slowly his wife arose. She crossed the room to the window, reached up and slowly drew open the shutters.[59]

Love is not love which changes when changes come. Love overcomes imperfections and absorbs them by grace. This is a touch of heaven on earth. It is the love which lasts forever because it is rooted in God's love which never dies.

A young husband stood at my door and asked, "What about life after death? I can't imagine not having my wife to love in heaven, and yet Jesus said there is no marriage in heaven" (Luke 20:35). It is a good question and quite natural that we should want to preserve a loving relationship forever. Moreover, no matter how much we love and are loved in marriage in this life, we have a feeling that somehow we are just getting started. A man walked away from his wife's grave saying, "I know there must be a heaven because wherever she is, is heaven."

In previous chapters we have said that marriage is a school and a signpost and a touch of heaven. No matter how great and fulfilling a marriage may be it always points beyond itself. Indeed, this may be one of its chief purposes. It is a taste of what is to come. It is given here so that we can begin to learn what love is, and grace and forgiveness and patience and openness and freedom. In heaven all of this will be expanded and intensified. We won't need our physical bodies to communicate our love. Love will be pure and complete and not require the framework of marriage. So we will not love our spouse less but more, and everybody else also. We shall know as we are known, (I Corinthians 13:12) and love as we are loved.

A close friend to the Hunter clan for well over sixty years told us in a Christmas letter the sad news of the passing of his dear wife. After giving a beautiful tribute to her he wrote:

I do not mourn as one who has no hope. The first Christmas was the forerunner of the cruel cross, and the tears of a Mother; which in turn, was the prelude of the Resurrection and Christ's conquest over death.

And he ended:"THE FUTURE IS AS BRIGHT AS THE PROMISES OF GOD."

So we do not grieve as those who have no hope (I Thessalonians 4:13) because Christian marriage points us forward beyond death. God promises, "I will never leave you nor forsake you; I will be with you to the end" (Hebrews 13:5, Matthew 28:20). His love is always available, so persons can always be changed and marriages can always be remade. This is both the promise and the perfection of the marital state.

An unknown author put it in a nutshell:

I love you,
Not only for what you are,
But for what I am
When I am with you.

I love you,
Not only for what
You have made of yourself,
But for what
You are making of me.

I love you
For the part of me
That you bring out;
I love you
For putting your hand
Into the heaped-up heart
And passing over
All the foolish, weak things
That you can't help
Dimly seeing there,

And for drawing out
Into the light
All the beautiful belongings
That no one else had looked
Quite far enough to find.

I love you because you
Are helping me to make
Of the lumber of my life
Not a tavern
But a temple;
Out of the works
Of my every day
Not a reproach
But a song . . .

Christian marriage is an adventure into freedom, freedom that has found its one place of supreme allegiance, Jesus Christ. Bound to Him a couple cannot help but grow and mature as they bring out the best in each other and as together they explore and apply life's highest meanings and richest gifts.

To conclude the wedding ceremony, a certain clergyman prays these words over a couple who are kneeling, immediately after being pronounced man and wife:

O God of love, You have established marriage for our welfare and happiness. It is Your plan and only with You can we work it out with joy. Our joys are doubled since the happiness of one is the happiness of the other. And our burdens are halved since when we share them we divide the load.

Bless this husband. May his strength be his wife's protection, his character her pride, and may he so live that she will find in him the haven for which the heart of a woman truly longs.

Bless this wife. Give her a tenderness that will make her great, deep understanding and deep faith in You. Give her the inner beauty of soul that never fades, that eternal youth that is found in holding fast the things that never age.

Give them great spiritual purpose in life. May they not expect perfection of each other that belongs alone to You. May they minimize each other's weaknesses, be swift to praise and see each other through a lover's kind and patient eyes.

Give them enough tears to keep them tender, enough hurts to keep them humane, enough failure to keep their hands clenched tightly in Yours and enough success to make them sure they walk with You.

May they always experience that breathless wonder that exclaims, ''Out of all this world you have chosen me.''

And when life is done and the sun is setting, may they be found then as now still hand in hand, still thanking You for each other, until at last one shall lay the other into Your loving arms. This we pray through Jesus Christ.

AMEN

REFERENCES

1. *Toronto Star,* February 8, 1974, p. A9.
2. H.D. Lewis, *The Spectator,* Nov. 28, 1964, p. 15.
3. Prof. Vello Sermat, *Toronto Star,* September 18, 1971, pp. 19-35.
4. Faye Dunaway, *Toronto Star,* September 18, 1971, p. 19.
5. H.D. Lewis, *The Spectator,* Nov. 28, 1964, p. 15.
6. *Life,* March 30, 1959.
7. *Christian Century,* August 27, 1980.
8. A. Miller, "With Respect For Her Agony—But With Love," *Life,* February 7, 1964.
9. *Guilt and Grace,* (Harper and Row: New York, 1962), pp. 80-81.
10. Nicol Williamson, *People,* February 21, 1977, p. 96.
11. Tom Wolfe, New Scenes From A Marriage, *Quest,* September 1978, p. 31.
12. *Guilt and Grace,* p. 85.
13. Wes Seeliger, "Fight Like A Dog," *Faith At Work,* September 1976, p. 23.
14. Robert Thomas Allen, "I'm Sick of Sex," *Reader's Digest Reader,* 1951, p. 92.
15. M.B. Ray, *How Never To Be Tired,* (McLelland and Stewart: Toronto, 1944), p. 79.
16. *Mere Christianity,* (Geoffrey Bles: London), p. 108.
17. *Transposition and Other Addresses,* Chapter Two.
18. *Ibid.*
19. *The Four Loves, (Geoffrey Bles: London, 1960),* pp. 2 and 11.
20. "The House of Christmas," quoted from *The Questing Spirit,* Luccock and Brentano, (Coward-McCann, Inc.: New York, 1947), p. 353.
21. *Sojourners,* October 1982, p. 16.
22. *The New Demons* (Seabury Press, 1973), p. 76.
23. *The Oxford Dictionary of Quotations* (London, 1941), p. 190.
24. Eva Drobot, *Homemakers,* March 1978.
25. John Yungblut, *"Sex and The Human Psyche,"* Pendle Hill Pamphlet, No. 203.
26. *Vancouver Sun,* March 29, 1982.
27. *Faith at Work* (Hawthorn Books Inc., 1958).
28. David and Vera Mace.

29. September, 1975.

30. Quoted from Elizabeth Achtemeier, *The Committed Marriage* (Westminister Press: Philadelphia, 1976), p. 124.

31. Roland Bainton, *Here I stand* (Abingdon-Cokesbury Press: Nashville, 1950), pp. 300-301.

32. Stanley Jones, *Christian Maturity* (Abingdon, 1957), p. 345.

33. *Christian Century,* May 18, 1949, p. 625.

34. Anna Mow, *Your Teenager and You* (Zondervan: Grand Rapids, Michigan, 1967), p. 82.

35. Thomas Harris, *I'm O.K. - You're O.K.* (Harper and Row: New York, 1967), p. 236.

36. *Springs of Creative Living* (Abingdon Cokesbury: Nashville, 1940), p. 13.

37. Don and Marjorie Olds, ''After the Honeymoon,'' *Faith At Work,* October 1975, p. 6.

38. Joanne and Lew Koch, ''The Urgent Drive To Make Good Marriages Better,'' *Psychology Today,* September 1976, p. 83.

39. Dr. Frank Sommers, ''Till Divorce Us Do Part,'' *MacLeans,* April 19, 1976, p. 26.

40. *Toronto Star,* November 12, 1974.

41. Doris Hopper, *Toronto Star,* January 3, 1978, p. D1.

42. ''The New Morality,'' *Time,* November 21, 1977, p. 68.

43. *Ibid.*

44. *Ibid.*

45. Mary Johnson, *People,* July 1980, p. 51.

46. Lucille Ball, ''Our Second Wedding,'' *Guideposts,* May 1954, p. 1.

47. *The Four Loves,* p. 109.

48. Sally Quinn, ''Why I Decided To Marry,'' *Toronto Star,* February 15, 1981, p. C21.

49. Paul Nowack, ''Till Divorce Do Us Part,'' *MacLeans,* April 19, 1976, p. 26.

50. ''Hite-ing Back,'' *Time,* December 12, 1977, p. 64.

51. Philip Nobile, ''Speaking Out,'' *Us,* December 13, 1977, p. 17.

52. Jessyca Russell Gaver, ''Someone To Be Quiet With,'' *Guideposts,* November 1977, P. 26.

53. *Stress Without Distress,* Lippincott Co., Philadelphia, 1974, p. 78.

54. Charles Shedd, *Letters to Karen, Reader's Digest Book Condensation,* January 1966, p. 15.

55. *Abundant Living* (Abingdon Press: Nashville, 1942), p. 293.

56. Isodore Rubin quoting Dr. G. Lombard Kelly in *Sexual Life After Sixty,* (Basic Books: New York, 1965), p. 99.

57. *Ibid:* p. 164.

58. Nancy Roberts, ''Living Life As A Gift,'' *Faith At Work,* August 1972, p. 6.

59. Galen Drake, ''Fragile Moments,'' *Guideposts,* January 1966, p. 29.